Gill Books
Hume Avenue, Park West, Dublin 12

www.gillbooks.ie

Gill Books is an imprint of M.H. Gill & Co.

ISBN: 978-0-7171-8598-6

This book was created and produced by Teapot Press Ltd

Text by Richard Killeen
Edited by Fiona Biggs
Designed by Tony Potter & Becca Wilde
Picture research by Joe Potter & Tony Potter

Printed in Europe

This book is typeset in Dax and Minion Pro

A CIP catalogue record for this book is available
from the British Library.

5 4 3 2 1

A POCKET HISTORY OF
NORTHERN IRELAND

Richard Killeen

Gill Books

Contents

Contents

Map showing the four provinces and 32 counties of Ireland.

NORTHERN IRELAND

Donegal
Derry
Antrim
Tyrone
Belfast
Fermanagh
Armagh
Down
Monaghan
Sligo
Leitrim
Cavan
Mayo
Roscommon
Louth
Longford
Meath
Westmeath
Dublin
Galway
Offaly
Kildare
REPUBLIC OF IRELAND
Laois
Wicklow
Clare
Carlow
Tipperary
Kilkenny
Limerick
Wexford
Kerry
Waterford
Cork

Ulster
Connacht
Leinster
Munster

Background

The remote origins of Northern Ireland go back to the 17th century, when England finally conquered the Gaelic chieftains of Ulster, the last Irish province to resist subjection. The defeated chieftains were harried into exile and their lands declared forfeit to the crown. There followed a huge plantation of Anglo-Scots settlers on the lands thus vacated. The plantation continued for most of the 17th century and was one the biggest – if not the biggest – voluntary transfer of population in contemporary Europe.

The settlers were Protestants, the Scots mainly Calvinist or Presbyterian, the English Anglican. The remaining Gaelic tenants,

Jan van Huchtenburgh, *Battle of the Boyne between James II and William III, 11 June 1690.*

who were still numerous, were doggedly Roman Catholic. In an age when religion was a key marker of loyalty and political allegiance, this mattered.

Protestants and Catholics in Ulster never cohered. There were atrocities, sieges, wars. When the dust finally settled in the 1690s, the Protestants had established their superiority. Within the overall Protestant community, English Anglicans were the dominant element. This caused resentment among the Presbyterians, whose numbers were greater. Although they suffered some political disabilities, these were not as great as those imposed on Roman Catholics.

In 1798, there was a brief attempt at a Presbyterian–Catholic alliance, but this faded quickly in the wake of military defeat. After that, the Protestant–Catholic divide resumed and became absolute. The more Protestant east of Ulster industrialised in the 19th century, becoming one of industrial Britain's powerhouses. The most consequential event in the more Catholic west – and in the rest of Ireland – was the Great Famine of 1845–52, the last major subsistence crisis in Western Europe. The contrast between Protestant wealth and Catholic misery could hardly have been starker.

The potato famine of 1845.

Unionism

In 1801, Ireland had been fully integrated into the United Kingdom, having previously been a semi-autonomous sister kingdom. The three southern Catholic provinces and the Catholic population of Ulster grew increasingly unhappy with the Union.

By the 1880s, they had succeeded in getting home rule or devolution of domestic powers on the British political agenda. For Ulster Protestants, this was an existential threat: they feared Catholic dominance.

The immediate crisis passed but by the early years of the 20th century, the danger loomed again. A Liberal government was elected in 1905, formally committed to Irish home rule although with a sufficiently large parliamentary majority to ignore Irish demands for the moment.

Still, the danger was perceived as real. There was a coherent bloc of Irish nationalist MPs at Westminster, whose principal demand was home rule. If they were to hold the balance of power in a hung parliament – as was to happen in 1910 – then they could barter their support for Irish devolution.

In 1905, the Ulster Unionist Council (UUC) was formed in Belfast to act as a central clearing house for all Irish unionist political activity.

But, as the name implied, its focus was principally on Ulster, where Protestant numbers were greatest. Out of it emerged a disciplined Irish Unionist Party, dedicated to resisting home rule for the entire island.

The UUC coordinated and consolidated all unionist political activity in the province. It gingered up local associations, made sure that supporters were registered to vote and established an efficient political machine on the ground throughout the province.

Edward Carson depicted on a rare unionist postcard of 1912.

The Third Home Rule Bill

In 1910, the worst fears of the unionists were realised. A general election left the Irish Nationalist Party holding the balance of parliamentary power. They demanded home rule in return for supporting Asquith's Liberal government.

This caused one of the greatest constitutional crises in British history. The Tory opposition was bitterly opposed to any concessions to Irish nationalism, because they viewed such concessions as a fracturing of the British metropolitan state and thus a betrayal of the constitutional order. Previous attempts to legislate for Irish home rule had been doomed to fail in the solidly Tory House of Lords, but now, the Liberals – under Irish nationalist pressure – forced through the Parliament Act 1911, neutering the Lords' veto and replacing it with a mere delaying power of two years.

There followed the Home Rule Bill of 1912, the third such attempt in less than 30 years. This time, with the Lords' veto gone and a secure parliamentary majority, it seemed certain to succeed. The third Home Rule Bill proposed a

Herbert Henry Asquith, first Earl of Oxford and Asquith, was a British statesman and Liberal politician who served as prime minister of the United Kingdom between 1908 and 1916.

subordinate Dublin parliament with limited domestic powers but with major financial, military and diplomatic powers retained in London. Ireland would still be a part of the United Kingdom.

None of this mattered to those opposed to home rule, who saw in it only a fatal wound to the British constitution. That opposition was intense in London, but in Ulster, it was ferocious. Finally, the great existential threat was upon Ulster unionists. It was time to organise.

Chorus:- "OH! HENRY WHERE DID YOU GET THAT CIGAR & WHY ARE YOU SMOKING IT? YOU'LL CHOKE US ALL."

H.C.B.   CAN'T HELP IT, REDMOND SAYS "I MUST SMOKE IT".

Home Rule cartoon.

Craig & Carson

Sir James Craig emerged gradually as the principal organiser of the Ulster Unionist Council. Born in 1871, he was the son of a wealthy distiller. Fuelled by his father's money, he went into politics and was elected to Westminster in 1906 for the safe unionist seat of East Down.

Sir James Craig.

Unionism throughout Ireland – not least in Ulster – had traditionally looked to the landed, aristocratic element for political leadership. This continued to be the position in the three southern provinces, where the Protestant mercantile middle class was small. But in Ulster, buoyed by the fortunes made in the Industrial Revolution, it was large, assertive and self-confident. Moreover, it was disproportionately Presbyterian, not Anglican, which was a distinction that mattered.

Although he was principally focused on Ulster, the person Craig manoeuvred into the leadership of the Irish Unionist Party in 1910 wanted to save all of Ireland for the Union. His name was Edward Carson. Craig was a charmless organiser. Carson was charismatic and slightly hysterical. Their complementary skills and attributes made them a formidable team.

Carson was a Dubliner. A lawyer, he first came to notice as crown prosecutor during the land agitation of the 1880s. He later established himself at the English Bar, where his most famous hour was the destruction of Oscar Wilde, and in Conservative politics. In the 1906 election he survived a rout of the Conservatives, leaving him as one of the most prominent figures on the opposition benches. Still in his early 50s, he might have harboured thoughts of even higher things in a future Tory government. Instead, he accepted Craig's offer of the leadership of the Irish Unionist Party in 1910.

Edward Carson making a speech.

Ulster Day, 1912

All through the summer of 1912, as the Home Rule Bill was making its way through Westminster, James Craig galvanised unionist Ulster in a series of meetings. The bill had been introduced in April. In Britain itself, the Conservatives were utterly opposed to it: their leader, Andrew Bonar Law, the son of an Ulster Presbyterian minister, spoke in highly inflammatory terms – touching on treason – at a huge rally at Blenheim Palace in July.

The summer was marked by a number of grossly sectarian outrages across Ulster, all of which conspired to raise the political temperature. In September, Carson spoke at a series of mass meetings across the province, starting in the west in County Fermanagh and moving steadily east towards Belfast and the planned Ulster Day, 28 September. That day, in the Ulster Hall, there was a religious service which both Carson and Craig attended, followed by a huge procession to Belfast City Hall.

Andrew Bonar Law.

There, Carson was the first person to sign the Ulster Solemn League and Covenant, a pledge to resist home rule by any and all means. Thereafter, bands from all over the city converged on City Hall and marchers in huge numbers signed the covenant in turn.

The Belfast proceedings were echoed right across Protestant Ulster. In all, 471,414 people signed a copy of the document. It was a dramatically public show of defiance. The apparently irresistible force of home rule had met with the immovable object of unionist resistance. Where was all this going?

The Ulster Covenant was issued in protest against the Third Home Rule Bill in September 1912.

The UVF, the Curragh, Larne & Howth

All through 1910 and 1911, as home rule became ever more a reality, militant Ulster Protestants under the aegis of the Ulster Unionist Council (UUC) began to form local militias. Arms were imported, secretly and illegally. By the time Ulster Day came around in September 1912, it was estimated that these militias aggregated to more than 100,000 men.

They were formalised as the Ulster Volunteer Force (UVF) in January 1913. Their military leadership included retired British army officers. In April 1914, they pulled off an audacious coup when they

Members of the UVF.

landed 25,000 rifles and about three million rounds of ammunition from Germany at Larne, County Antrim. The authorities looked the other way. Ulster was preparing to resist Irish home rule, by force of arms, if necessary.

A month earlier, 60 British officers stationed at the Curragh, near Dublin, had threatened to resign their commissions if the army was deployed to quash a possible resistance movement in Ulster. It was tantamount to mutiny, the first such threat any British government had faced since 1688.

Worse still, a month after Larne, the Irish Volunteers, a nationalist militia, landed arms at Howth, just north of Dublin. This time, there was no blind eye turned by the authorities. In the subsequent fracas, four civilians died, shot by British troops in the city centre.

A conference was held in Buckingham Palace in July 1914 to try to square the Irish circle: the nationalist demand for home rule versus Ulster resistance, possibly armed. It failed. The Home Rule Act was passed in September but suspended, because in the meantime the First World War had broken out.

King George V invited the leaders of Irish nationalism and Irish unionism to discuss plans to introduce home rule to Ireland and avert a feared civil war.

The First World War, the Easter Rising & the Somme

The war transformed the situation and provided the indispensable context for all that followed. The UVF was formed into a regular British army division, the 36th Ulster, and suffered catastrophic losses on the Somme.

HIGNETT'S CIGARETTES.

JOHN REDMOND.

John Redmond pictured on a cigarette card.

The war split the Irish Volunteers; most supported the war effort, at the bidding of John Redmond, the leader of the Irish Parliamentary Party that had just delivered home rule. But a minority refused to fight and the movement split, the majority now calling themselves the National Volunteers and the militant minority retaining the old name.

A minority of that minority then tripped off the Easter Rising of 1916, the most transformative event in modern Irish history. They were out-and-out republicans for whom home rule was not enough. They fought for a fully independent republic, severed

Irish troops in a First World War trench.

from Britain. Their fight stood in sharp contrast to the fate of the 36th Ulster, butchered on the Somme a few weeks later. If Ulster wouldn't swallow home rule, what was it supposed to make of a republic?

By the end of the war, Sinn Féin had emerged as the radical alternative to home rule and swept all before it on the nationalist side. A further futile conference tried to break the impasse and, predictably, failed. A general election in December 1918 showed nationalist Ireland solid for Sinn Féin and Protestant Ulster as firmly unionist as ever.

The War of Independence & Partition

Sinn Féin won 73 of the 105 Irish seats in the general election. Instead of attending Westminster, they formed themselves into an Irish parliament, the Dáil, which met in Dublin for the first time on 21 January 1919. On the same day, the first fatal shots were fired in the Irish War of Independence, a guerrilla campaign that ran on for two and a half years and further radicalised the nationalist demand.

The events of the previous five years had rendered Redmond's Home Rule Act a dead letter. In 1920, the government of David Lloyd George introduced a fourth home rule bill. Its provisions were stillborn in the South, where events were nearly out of British control. However, under the title of the Government of Ireland Act 1920, it became law. It partitioned Ireland. A subsequent treaty with Sinn Féin ended the War of Independence but confirmed partition.

Ulster itself was split by these arrangements. The historic province comprised nine counties but the unionists claimed only six,

Carson and Redmond.

those which yielded a solid, reliable Protestant majority. Thus Northern Ireland was born.

Nationalists were outraged by partition, especially those now trapped in the six counties, but for radical nationalists, the achievement of full republican status was more immediately important. In this, they failed – at least for the moment. Partition, which many thought must be temporary, proved more resilient. It was a bitter blow for southern unionists. Edward Carson was a disappointed man. James Craig was not: he was now the first prime minister of Northern Ireland.

RIC and military leaving Limerick.

Two States

From December 1922, there were two states on the island of Ireland. Its thirty-two counties were partitioned. Twenty-six counties – nationalist Ireland – became the Irish Free State, a dominion within the British Commonwealth; it later evolved into the Republic of Ireland. The six counties of Northern Ireland remained within the United Kingdom, with a devolved government and administration in Belfast.

A short but nasty civil war broke out in the Free State between those who accepted the treaty settlement with Britain and those who held out for full republican status. The government won, but not before losing its charismatic strong man, Michael Collins, to a sniper's bullet. Collins had been a vocal opponent of Northern Ireland because of ill-treatment of its Catholic minority. He had organised a boycott of Belfast goods, more a symbolic gesture than anything substantial, but evidence of the clear hostility between the two new entities.

There were meetings between Craig and Collins and also between Craig and Éamon de Valera, the political head of Irish republicanism and soon to be the most consequential figure in Irish political life, although temporarily eclipsed when he adopted the losing position in the civil war. These meetings achieved little or nothing, other than to clarify the gulf of misunderstanding between the two sides. But the Free State had one great hope: under the terms of the treaty with Britain, there was to be a Boundary Commission, which they felt sure would weaken Northern Ireland – perhaps fatally – by transferring large nationalist enclaves in the south and west to the South.

Cartoon from 1920s.
The Kindest Cut of All
Welsh Wizard: *'I will now proceed to cut this map in two parts and place them in the hat. After a suitable interval they will be found to have come together of their own accord – (ASIDE) – at least I hope so; I've never done this trick before.'*

Communal Violence

Northern Ireland was born in violence. In effect, the all-island civil war that had threatened to break out in 1914 but was forestalled by the First World War, now came to pass in Ulster.

Cathal Brugha, Chief of Staff of the Irish Republican Army from 1917 to 1919.

In two years – July 1920 to July 1922 – 557 people were killed in communal violence in Northern Ireland; 303 were Catholics, 172 Protestants and 82 members of the police force and army. In Belfast, the Catholic population comprised only 25 per cent of the total, yet it bore 62 per cent of the fatalities. In addition, more than 10,000 Catholics lost their jobs – often forced out with menaces by their Protestant co-workers – and more than 20,000 were rendered homeless.

The fatalities among Protestants and the security forces were due to a concerted campaign by the IRA to strangle the new statelet at birth. It was rather like a regional version of the southern War of Independence, except that it was being waged against a new political entity, just established, in which the authorities held by far the stronger hand.

This campaign confirmed for Protestants – as if any such further confirmation were required – that Northern Ireland's Catholic and nationalist minority was a relentless fifth column. This view, by no means incorrect, influenced much of what followed over the next 50 years. Protestant paranoia had a long history in Ulster. It now took another twist in a downward spiral.

Michael Collins on his deathbed, by John Lavery.

Michael Collins is killed in an ambush in 1922.

Derry, 1920

The initial outbreak of violence had begun in Derry in 1920, even before the formal partition of the island. Derry was a special case. In Protestant mythology, it was the Maiden City, the heroic unviolated walled town that had held out – against all odds – when besieged by the Catholic army of King James II in 1689. Although that might have seemed a time long distant from 1920, in Ulster it wasn't.

The armed merchant ship *Mountjoy* breaks through the defensive boom to relieve the Siege of Derry.

In the course of the 19th century, as Derry industrialised, its factories drew in people from the countryside looking for work. By the end of that century, it had a Catholic majority, having long since spread beyond the confinement of its historic walls. But a clever gerrymandering of the local ward boundaries ensured that the Protestant minority retained secure possession of the Londonderry Corporation.

In 1919, British legislation had introduced proportional representation for Irish local government elections. The following year, this ensured a nationalist majority on the Londonderry Corporation for the first time. Other majority-Catholic local authorities in west Ulster followed suit. In the early summer of 1920, violence in Derry claimed 40 lives before the British army, aligning itself in a partisan manner with the local UVF, restored a version of order.

After partition one of the earliest priorities of the devolved unionist government in Belfast was to reverse the decision regarding proportional representation for local government, thus restoring the status quo ante in Derry.

Troops called to restore order.

The Ulster Special Constabulary

In the last days before partition, Lloyd George's government in London approved the establishment of the Ulster Special Constabulary, a police reserve. It was little short of the UVF re-formed (but not reformed). There were three categories, A, B and C, of which the B Specials were the ones that mattered and the most numerous, being almost 20,000 men in all.

They effectively acted as an aggressive militia in their local areas, carrying weapons that were supposed to be kept in police barracks when the men were off-duty. They were hated by Catholics from the day of their inception to that of their disbandment in 1970, and with good reason. They represented the local face of unionist rule at its harshest and most partisan, and they acquired a well-earned reputation for brutality and malignant ill-temper. The fact that each unit was local meant that, in small communities

Lloyd George.

where everyone knew everyone else, the intensity of the hatred between the Specials and those whom they harassed – their Catholic neighbours – could only grow.

In a sense, the B Specials symbolised the foundational dilemma of Northern Ireland. It was born in violence, as the IRA campaign tried to see it stillborn. Unionists knew that, even after the violence stopped, the IRA would try again later. They did, and the B Specials were a thorn in their side and helped defeat later campaigns. So, from a unionist perspective, the Specials justified their existence, but what sort of a place was it that needed a brutal militia of this sort?

Inspection of the B Specials.

The Northern Ireland Elections, 1921

The first general election to the new Northern Ireland parliament in Belfast City Hall – it did not move to the pompous grandeur of Stormont until 1932 – took place in May 1921. Although held under proportional representation (PR), it produced a 'bounce' for the Ulster Unionist Party led by James Craig: it won 77 per cent of the seats – 40 out of 52 – on 67 per cent of the popular vote. One way or another, it was a decisive win.

It proved the wisdom of partitioning along the lines of the six counties rather than all nine, with the historic province's near-Catholic majority quite likely to have deployed PR to their own benefit. Not that PR lasted long in the new Northern Ireland. In 1929 it was replaced by the old first-past-the-post system with single-member constituencies, guaranteeing unionist majorities.

Thus the pattern was set for Northern Ireland until the reforms forced upon it by the outbreak of the Troubles in the later 1960s and early 1970s. The state existed for the comfort and convenience of the Protestant and unionist majority. Catholics and nationalists were effectively second-class citizens, required to know their place. This state of affairs lasted

Sir James Craig.

for about 50 years, despite occasional outbreaks of sectarian violence and IRA activity. It seemed to be a kind of normality. The wonder is that it took so long for the sheer abnormality of Northern Ireland to show itself to the world.

The opening of the first Parliament of Northern Ireland by King George V at City Hall, Belfast, on 22 June 1921, following Northern Ireland's general election held on 24 May 1921. It was the first election to the Parliament of Northern Ireland. Ulster Unionist Party members won a two-thirds majority of votes cast and more than three-quarters of the seats in the assembly. The election took place during the Irish War of Independence, on the same day as the election to the parliament of Southern Ireland.

Violence Ends

The communal violence and the associated IRA campaign continued into 1922, with Northern Ireland now an established if nervous entity. The intensity of the campaign was highlighted by the damage to the properties of prominent unionists. In April, the total amount claimed in the courts for malicious damage to property was £252,578. In May, it was £794,678 and in June almost as much again at £760,018. In May, among the 90 people murdered in Belfast alone was the unionist MP W. J. Twaddell.

In April 1922, the Royal Ulster Constabulary (RUC) replaced the old Royal Irish Constabulary (RIC) as the main police force in Northern Ireland. In May, the devolution of security and policing powers was completed, and the Belfast administration now had the opportunity to do that which its every instinct told it to do: crack down hard. Police powers were extended, a general curfew was imposed, the B Specials were mobilised and the pubs were made to close early.

It worked. The IRA were defeated. It had not helped that the civil war in the Free State had drawn off resources and men from the Northern command, but the iron fist of the Belfast administration had contributed to the result. It was not a contest of equals: the new administration held by far the stronger hand and used it.

In July 1922, it was decided in Dublin to abandon the northern campaign. This was agreed with Michael Collins. Less than a month later Collins was dead and the civil war was resolved in favour of Collins's successor, W. T. Cosgrave, in May 1923. It seemed that Ireland, north and south, was at last at peace.

Police searching pedestrians at the scene of the murder of W. J. Twaddell.

The Special Powers Act

The keystone of the new get-tough policy was the Civil Authorities (Special Powers) Act, passed in April 1922. It gave the minister for home affairs powers so sweeping that they were without parallel in any other democracy. Under its principal provisions, the minister could arrest without warrant, intern without trial, prohibit coroners' inquests, order the flogging of prisoners or have special courts sentence them to death, expropriate property without compensation, prohibit any organisation and suppress public meetings and any publication of which he disapproved.

Special Powers Act 1922.

One unionist MP, George Hanna, complained that the act was too complicated and that it should simply state that the minister 'shall have the power to do whatever he likes, or let someone else do whatever he likes for him'. This was not said in jest, although it was very nearly a pithy summary of the legislation.

The act remained in place, with a series of renewals before eventually being made permanent, until the early 1970s, when it was replaced under the pressure of the early Troubles and the various reforms forced on Belfast by London.

At the end of the civil war in the South, the government employed emergency legislation as drastic as the Special Powers Act – even to the point of executing 77 republican prisoners in cold blood, something the Belfast government never contemplated. But the new Dublin government was fundamentally legitimate in the eyes of all its citizens; the Belfast government was illegitimate in the eyes of its large minority.

Sir Richard Dawson Bates, first minister for home affairs and a member of the Privy Council of Northern Ireland. He stood accused of intervening to ensure that prison sentences were not imposed on Protestants who attacked Catholics, and of gerrymandering.

The Boundary Commission

Members of the Boundary Commission, left to right: Francis Bernard Bourdillon, J. R. Fisher (Northern Ireland), Mr Justice Feetham (Chairman), Dr Eoin MacNeill (Free State representative), and C. Beerstacher (private secretary to Mr Justice Feetham).

Although northern nationalists had lost the various battles that accompanied the establishment of Northern Ireland, they had one remaining hope. This was the Boundary Commission agreed between the Free State and the British government under the Anglo-Irish Treaty of December 1921.

The nationalist hope was that large areas on the periphery of the territory, containing substantial local Catholic majorities, would be transferred to the Free State, thus enfeebling the residual Northern Ireland and perhaps rendering it unviable.

It all proved to be a damp squib. Craig refused to have anything to do with it. The Dublin government sent Eoin MacNeill, himself originally from the North, a scholar of some distinction and now minister for education in the Free State. A unionist journalist, J. R. Fisher, stood in for the Belfast government and the chairman was a South African judge, Mr Justice Feetham. The judge's role was obviously crucial and he tended to interpret his brief fairly narrowly. The commissioners considered 130 written submissions and examined 585 witnesses without reaching any conclusion that suggested substantial change. A few minor border adjustments were proposed, nothing more.

In November 1925, this stalemate was leaked to the London press. MacNeill resigned. Some northern nationalists had hoped that all of Counties Fermanagh and Tyrone would be transferred south, so the sense of disappointment was acute. It was matched by relief on the unionist side. Everyone now decided to look the other way and do nothing. Things remained as they were. The boundaries of Northern Ireland were finally delineated.

Education

The seventh Marquess of Londonderry, a direct descendant of the great Castlereagh, was an improbable choice as minister of education in Craig's government. A grandee standing at the very apex of London high society, he was an oddity in Northern Ireland despite his Ulster roots. In 1923, he attempted to institute a primary school system on non-denominational lines. This did indeed unite Protestants and Catholics, but only in bitter opposition to Lord Londonderry's plans.

The clergy on both sides were the school managers. The Catholics made it clear from the start that the schooling of Catholics could only take place in Catholic schools with a Catholic ethos under the direction of Catholic teachers. The Catholic teachers were even more adamant; for a while, they refused to draw their salaries from Belfast and were paid emergency salaries direct from Dublin instead. Nor did Catholics make any representations to a committee set up to advise Londonderry: this was part of a recurring pattern whereby nationalists simply boycotted and ignored the institutions of Northern Ireland.

Under Londonderry's legislation, school management was removed from clergy and transferred to a series of boards. This was a dead letter on the Catholic side but reluctantly accepted on the Protestant side until a revolt of teachers, parents and clergy caused Craig to reverse Londonderry's plans and restore what was in effect the sectarian status quo. Londonderry naturally resigned. The education system remained absolutely segregated by religion. It set a pattern that persists to this day.

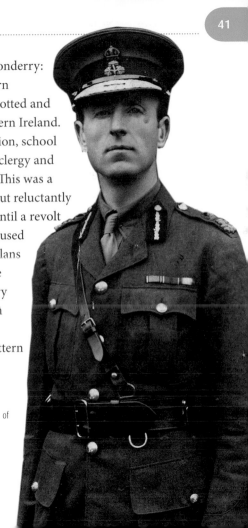

Charles Vane-Tempest-Stewart, seventh Marquess of Londonderry.

Franchise

Right from the start, Northern Ireland was geographically unbalanced. The Protestant majority was concentrated east of the River Bann, which flowed south to north not quite through the middle of the province. The larger area west of the Bann was less densely populated than the east but it contained substantial local Catholic and nationalist majorities.

The Belfast parliament passed an act robbing any local authority of its powers should it fail to exercise them. This happened in County Fermanagh where a nationalist-controlled council pulled down the Union flag from the courthouse in Enniskillen and instead pledged allegiance to Dublin. In all, 21 local authorities in the south and west of the province were dissolved for similar conduct.

These manifestations of disloyalty led to unionist pressure to scrap proportional representation in local elections. This was done in short order. With the return of the straight vote came the old

Opposite:
The Peace Bridge that crosses the River Foyle, joining the Protestant Waterside to the Catholic Cityside in Derry.

gerrymandering of constituencies with Catholic majorities. Despite satisfactory victories for the unionists in the general elections of 1921 and 1925, they got rid of PR for general elections as well in 1929. Now all electoral contests – for local government and parliament alike – in Northern Ireland were held under the straight vote, with the constituency and ward boundaries drawn to maximum unionist advantage.

It copper-fastened the logic of choosing six counties over nine to mark the boundary of Northern Ireland. Within this area, the minority could be contained, not least because Catholic educational attainments were much lower than Protestant and the Catholic middle class was small.

Gerrymandering

Derry, the second city of Northern Ireland, was its most notorious example of gerrymandering. It had long had a Catholic majority but was regarded as sacred soil by Protestants because of its heroic success in defending itself against Catholic besiegers way back in 1689. They were determined to control the small city, Catholic majority or not.

Three wards were created of unequal size but equal representation. The Catholic majority were corralled in one huge ward while the Protestants were divided into two wards. This meant that the unionist minority elected a majority to Derry Corporation. A similar pattern was repeated throughout west Ulster. Unionists claimed that rateable valuation was the standard test for the franchise in British local elections and that unionists, being generally richer, were therefore entitled to the representation they received. Nevertheless, the effect of gerrymandering and the straight vote was unambiguous: 12 councils that had been nationalist-controlled before 1922 reverted safely to the unionist fold.

All this was done after the deliberations of an enquiry, led by a judge, which was yet again boycotted by nationalists. The result was that local unionists, egged on by Richard Dawson Bates, Minister for Home Affairs, were able to make their own arrangements. Subsequent nationalist complaints drew the response that they had only themselves to blame for not turning up. But it was hard to blame them: they knew the game was rigged from the start. As for Westminster, it looked the other way. Having 'solved' the Irish problem, it didn't want to know.

The Ulster Cabinet of 1920. Richard Dawson Bates is first on the left.

The 1929 General Election

Once the process of boundary adjustments and the reversion to the straight vote was completed, the new arrangements were tested in the 1929 general election. With complete predictability, it produced the goods for the unionists. Once again, they took 40 seats out of 52, the same as under PR eight years earlier.

Eleven nationalists were returned, all of them for constituencies either west of the Bann or touching the border with the Free State. The remaining seat went to the Northern Ireland Labour Party, which drew its support mainly from the Protestant community. As such, it was a constant object of suspicion to unionists, who saw it as a dangerous element – incipiently socialist in the eyes of the unionist leadership, all Tories – who would draw Protestant votes away from their true electoral home.

Belfast News-Letter, with advice on how to vote.

Following the disappointments of the Boundary Commission, some nationalists had taken their seats in the Belfast parliament. By 1932, they were so frustrated by serial unionist rejections and dismissals of their concerns, that Joe Devlin, their leader, led all of them out of parliament, where they remained for the rest of the decade.

It meant that from that moment on, there was unanimity in the Belfast parliament – now moved to Stormont, safe in Protestant East Belfast – for opinions loyal to the union with the rest of the United Kingdom. Craig had it all his own way. The Catholic minority – about one-third of the population – was effectively ignored.

Sir James Craig on an election poster.

ULSTER IS OURS

WHAT WE HAVE WE HOLD

A Protestant Parliament

Now ennobled as Viscount Craigavon, James Craig stated in the course of a parliamentary debate on minority rights: 'Since we took up office we have tried to be absolutely fair towards all the citizens of Northern Ireland. Actually, on an Orange platform, I myself laid down the principle, to which I still adhere, that I was prime minister not of one section of the community but of all, and that as far as I possibly could I was going to see that fair play was meted out to all classes and creeds without any favour whatever on my part.'

One of his backbenchers then said: 'What about your Protestant Parliament?' Craigavon replied: 'The hon. Member must remember that in the South they boasted of a Catholic State. They still boast of Southern Ireland being a Catholic State. All I boast of is that we are a Protestant Parliament and a Protestant State. It would be rather interesting for historians of the future to compare a Catholic State launched in the South with a Protestant State launched in the North and to see which gets on the better and prospers the more. It is most interesting for me at the moment to watch how they are progressing. I am doing my best always to top the bill and to be ahead of the South.' It was a blatant statement of the obvious, not least for being preceded by the self-deception of his opening remarks. In the new Northern Ireland, Catholics were simply not part of the people.

Punch cartoon.
President Cosgrave:
You are very obstinate.
Sir James Craig:
Well, so are you.
President Cosgrave:
I daren't be anything else.
Sir James Craig:
Same with me.

Sir Basil Brooke

The Brooke family had been in west Ulster since before the Plantation. The first of them, Basil Brooke (1567–1633) was an English army captain granted extensive lands by Queen Elizabeth I in what became County Fermanagh. The family prospered and the name Basil went down the generations until the latest in the line was born in 1888. The Brookes were a classic marcher, military family, holding lands at the periphery of the state for the crown.

The Brooke family crest on the fireplace in the Great Hall of the derelict Donegal Castle, home to the family until the 1670s.

Sir Basil Brooke had a good First World War, winning both the Military Cross and the Croix de Guerre. He was elected to the Belfast parliament in 1929 and was appointed minister of agriculture in 1933. He was charming but unambiguously sectarian. A local newspaper report of one of his parliamentary speeches made this clear:

'There was a great number of Protestants and Orangemen who employed Roman Catholics.

Sir Basil Brooke.

He felt he could speak freely on this subject as he had not a Roman Catholic about his own place [Cheers]. He appreciated the great difficulty experienced by some of them in procuring suitable Protestant labour, but he would point out that the Roman Catholics were endeavouring to get in everywhere and were out with all their force and might to destroy the power and constitution of Ulster … He would appeal to loyalists, therefore, wherever possible to employ good Protestant lads and lassies.'

Ten years later, he was prime minister of Northern Ireland.

Economic Woes

The end of the First World War brought an economic recession. Two of Northern Ireland's key industries, linen and shipbuilding, suffered badly. In 1929, the Wall Street Crash unleashed the greatest international economic crisis of the 20th century. Few places were immune, but Northern Ireland, overly dependent on exports of a limited range of goods to imperial markets, was

particularly hard hit. Shipbuilding shed 90 per cent of its workforce between 1924 and 1933. The following year, Workman Clark – 'the wee yard', smaller rival to Harland & Wolff – closed. By 1932, the year Stormont opened, the unemployment rate was a staggering 28 per cent.

Belfast linen was a luxury item particularly prone to tariffs, which were now widely and disastrously applied worldwide in a vast game of beggar-my-neighbour. In 1927, there was only 6 per cent unemployment in the linen industry; by 1938, it was 56 per cent.

In parliament, Jack Beattie, a NILP MP, created ructions in parliament by shouting down Craigavon, saying that the government was ignoring the 78,000 unemployed who were starving. He grabbed the mace and flung it to the floor, for which indignity he was thrown out of the House, accompanied by his colleague Tommy Henderson. On the government benches, they sang 'God Save the King'.

The crisis effected a brief setting aside of sectarian animosity in favour of working-class solidarity. There were strikes and marches in the autumn of 1932, at one of which the band played the music-hall favourite, 'Yes, We Have No Bananas', being the most non-sectarian tune they knew.

In the aftermath of the Wall Street Stock Market Crash one investor attempts to sell his car. The crash was followed by the Great Depression, the worst economic crisis of modern times.

Riots

The non-sectarianism did not hold. The authorities made only minimal concessions – just enough to put a stop to any non-sectarianism – and normal service resumed. There was a series of inter-communal incidents in 1933 and 1934, which exploded into full-scale sectarian rioting in 1935. It was the resumption of what by now was a depressing pattern, especially in Belfast. That year brought the silver jubilee of King George V, a moment of celebration for Protestants. Inevitably, tensions rose in an atmosphere of triumphalism. To calm things down, Dawson Bates, the Minister of Home Affairs, banned all parades, including the Orange march on 12 July. However, pressure from the Orange Order forced him to reverse the ban and the march went ahead.

What followed was the worst outbreak of sectarian rioting since 1922. Over the next six weeks or so, eight Protestants and five Catholics were killed, houses were torched and more than 2,000 families were left homeless. The army was called in but even troops with fixed bayonets were insufficient to stop the mayhem. In general, Catholics came off worst, especially those in exposed areas surrounded by Protestants.

Far from being any kind of breakthrough or new beginning, the brief rapprochement of 1932 was exposed as a mere flash in the pan, although it subsequently became the stuff of legend and longing in socialist circles. Instead, the 1935 riots were – depressingly – the renewal of a tradition of sectarian violence that stretched back to the mid-19th century and which would prove a generation later to have lost none of its malignant potency.

A Rolls-Royce armoured car in York Street, Belfast, June 1935.

The 1937 Constitution

In the South, Éamon de Valera had come to power in the 1932 general election. Ever since 1917, he had been the dominant political figure in nationalist Ireland. He was the highest-ranking survivor of the 1916 Rising. His career went into temporary eclipse when he took the losing side in the Civil War of 1922–23, fought over the terms of the Anglo-Irish Treaty that established the Free State. However, he recovered and, once in power again after 1932, dominated Southern political life for a generation.

De Valera carefully unpicked as much of the Treaty settlement as he could. Specifically, he drafted a new constitution and got it approved by referendum in the shadow of the British constitutional crisis caused by the abdication of King Edward VIII. It claimed the entire island as the national territory, although allowing that laws passed in Dublin would apply only in the 26 counties 'pending reintegration of the national territory'.

This blunt territorial claim naturally alienated unionist opinion in Northern Ireland. Even worse, article 44 of the constitution recognised the 'special position' of the Roman Catholic Church as the faith of the majority of its citizens. It was tantamount to stating that the South was a Catholic state for a Catholic people. Together with the severe

Eamon de Valera

censorship, the compulsory teaching of the Irish language and the denial of individual conscience and autonomy in family planning and marital matters, it is hard to imagine a programme less likely to appeal to unionists or to facilitate the reunification that de Valera rhetorically desired.

Nationalist Dilemmas

Joseph Devlin was an Irish journalist and influential nationalist politician. He was an MP for the Irish Parliamentary Party in the House of Commons in London, and later a Nationalist Party MP in the Parliament of Northern Ireland.

The Nationalist Party in Northern Ireland was the last surviving rump of Redmond's party that had been superseded in the South by Sinn Féin in 1917. Within Northern Ireland, it faced internal opposition from republican and IRA-supporting candidates but still commanded the greater degree of electoral support among the Catholic community. However, it was in a political dead end. Its long-time leader, Joe Devlin, had withdrawn his members from Stormont in 1932 in protest against the unyielding refusal of the unionists to offer them any role in the political process. He died in 1934 and was succeeded by Cahir Healy, a Westminster MP for Fermanagh and Tyrone.

Abstention from Stormont and Westminster was the consuming issue for nationalists. For republicans, it was a core principle and an article of faith. They had sufficient influence to put pressure on mainstream nationalists to adopt that position, thus reconfirming Devlin's decision to withdraw from Stormont in 1932. More moderate and pragmatic voices, among them Healy's, thought this futile gesture effectively left Catholics without any meaningful political representation.

It was a dilemma that could never be resolved and that has clear echoes to this day. Nationalists were damned if they did and damned if they didn't. At Stormont, the unionist government had simply ignored them. At local government level, the abolition of PR and the gerrymandering of constituencies and wards left them grossly under-represented. Every way they turned, they faced a political wall.

Cahir Healy.

John Miller Andrews, second prime minister of Northern Ireland.

Basil Stanlake Brooke, first Viscount Brookeborough.

Northern Ireland on the Eve of the Second World War

By the end of the 1930s, unionists could console themselves with the thought that Northern Ireland was now firmly established. The effective exclusion of nationalist opinion from most of the public sphere had, however, rendered the government lazy and unresponsive.

Craigavon was taking life easy and spent much of his time travelling to various agreeable corners of the empire, leaving the machinery of government in the hands of Dawson Bates, a narrow-minded provincial. Craigavon died in November 1940, a unionist hero, and was briefly succeeded by J. M. Andrews, a nonentity who retained most of the old guard in the cabinet.

Andrews and Sir Basil Brooke had threatened to resign in 1938 over the terms of an Anglo-Irish trade agreement as it affected Northern Ireland. Their fear was that Dublin might have increased leverage and influence over the North's economy, still feeling the pressures of the decade-long recession. Craigavon, in one of his last major contributions, took personal charge of negotiations with London and received assurances sufficient to neutralise Andrews and Brooke. Part of his appeal to doubters on his own side was that any show of disunity with unionism could be disastrous, given the fragile nature of the international situation.

The nationalists railed against the wickedness of partition without being able to advance a single practical proposal to end it. So, for the next generation nationalism comprised little more than windy rhetoric punctuated by occasional outbreaks of republican violence. Northern Ireland was the perfect zero-sum game.

At the outset of the Second World War the United Kingdom controlled, to varying degrees, 25 per cent of the world's population, and 30 per cent of its land mass.

Northern Ireland in the Second World War

The long-threatened war arrived in 1939. In Dublin, de Valera immediately declared the South neutral, a policy heartily endorsed by northern nationalists. In an equal and opposite reaction, it outraged unionist opinion, for whom loyalty in time of war – of all times – was the very essence of their being. For nationalists, partition was the issue: as long as it persisted, there could be no question of supporting the British war effort. However, neutrality was exercised in practice with a serpentine tact typical of de Valera. In the famous phrase, it showed 'a certain consideration for Britain'. German pilots who baled out over the South were interned; RAF men in similar circumstances were slipped across the border.

The war helped to revive Northern Ireland's economy. Even before it broke out, Belfast had become a key centre for aircraft production, with Short Brothers and Harland & Wolff establishing a major production plant that employed 6,000 men by 1937. The Harland & Wolff shipyard came to life producing cruisers and aircraft carriers for the Royal Navy, as well as many smaller craft. Engineering works also geared up for wartime production.

Once war was declared, the Northern Ireland government's first move was to neutralise internal enemies. It interned 45 IRA men without trial. It was hardly without cause, as IRA contacts with Berlin were to prove. The ability of the Royal Navy and the RAF to operate from Northern Ireland bases made a material contribution to the British war effort, a point specifically acknowledged by Churchill. In addition, the province became a forward base for American troops in the approach to the D-Day landings.

Although the Irish Republic remained neutral during the Second World War, many of the Irish involved were part of the navy and kept guard over British waters.

The Bombing of Belfast

Corner of York Street and Lower Donegal Street, Belfast blitz – January 1941. On the night of 4–5 May the Luftwaffe dropped over 100,000 bombs and incendiaries on the city.

All the wartime production activity drew the attention of the Germans. The Northern Ireland authorities believed that Belfast was beyond the range of the Luftwaffe's bombers, so the city was utterly unprepared for the devastating bombing raids on the city in April and May 1941. With only seven anti-aircraft batteries and no searchlights, the city was effectively defenceless against air attacks. Official figures stated that 745 people were killed in the first raid alone; the true figure was probably nearer 1,000. Tens of thousands were rendered homeless or dependent on charity. War production was severely disrupted.

The Germans almost certainly missed their primary targets. The worst of the blitz fell not on the shipyard and the adjacent Short Brothers works but on the civilian population just north of this industrial zone. The result was a frightful toll of civilian casualties in the densely populated industrial suburbs. The central telephone exchange was destroyed, breaking a vital link to the mainland.

For two hours the raids continued and fires raged out of control. The city fire brigade could not cope; water mains had been damaged and the pressure reduced accordingly. Basil Brooke gave permission to request the assistance of fire brigades from the South. De Valera agreed immediately and 13 fire engines and 70 men were despatched northwards, to be greeted by scenes of biblical horror. The Luftwaffe came back in May, although this final raid accounted for only 191 deaths; many people had simply fled to the countryside.

Although Wilhelm Franz Canaris was a German admiral and chief of the Abwehr, the German military intelligence service, he was among military officers involved in opposition to the Nazi leadership. He was executed in Flossenbürg concentration camp for high treason towards the end of the war.

IRA-German Contacts

The nationalist population was ambiguous about the war. From the very beginning, there were reports of curfew restrictions being deliberately ignored in Catholic areas. Moreover, since early 1939, the IRA had organised a bombing campaign in Britain. There were 127 explosions in British cities, killing seven people and achieving nothing except the execution of two IRA men.

The chief of staff responsible for the campaign was Seán Russell, a Dublin 1916 veteran. In 1940, he found himself in Berlin, where he attempted to gain German support for his campaign. It is unclear if Russell was pro-Nazi – although some in the IRA certainly had Nazi sympathies – or was simply operating on the principle that my enemy's enemy is my friend. In Russell's case, it hardly mattered: he met Admiral Canaris, who arranged to return him to Ireland by U-boat. En route, Russell died of a perforated ulcer and was buried at sea. Contacts between the IRA and the Germans continued. A few inept German spies arrived in the South and were quickly rounded up.

In Northern Ireland, meanwhile, the new local IRA commander, Hugh McAteer, started a sabotage campaign. Policemen were killed and wounded. After a gun battle in Belfast, six IRA men – including Joe Cahill, later highly influential in the post-1968 Troubles – were captured and sentenced to death. All but one, Tom Williams, who was hanged in September 1942, had their sentences commuted. The campaign resumed but, as ever, the authorities held the stronger hand. Over 300 men, including McAteer, were rounded up and interned. The IRA were neutralised – but only for the moment.

RUC wanted poster.

Hugh McAteer addressing an Easter commemoration in Derry in the 1950s. Veteran republicans Tommy Mellon and Seán Keenan are on his left and right respectively.

Trading Neutrality for Unity

The government in Belfast faced a potentially existential threat far greater than that which the IRA could offer. In May and June 1940, British fortunes in the war were at their lowest ebb: France had fallen, meaning that U-boat attacks in the Atlantic could be launched from bases in Brittany. The Battle of the Atlantic ensued and Churchill, newly installed as prime minister, bitterly regretted the handing back of three ports in Ireland under the terms of an agreement with de Valera in 1938. They had originally been retained by Britain under the 1922 Treaty.

Lord Halifax.

The question was put to the cabinet in London by Lord Halifax: should Irish unity be offered in return for the abandonment of Irish neutrality and the reopening of the ports to the Royal Navy? Churchill agreed and Malcolm MacDonald, the former dominions secretary, whom Churchill personally despised but who had good relations with de Valera, was deputed to sound out the Dublin authorities. All this was done behind Craigavon's back. When he discovered what was afoot he was incandescent. It seems clear that both Churchill and his predecessor Chamberlain had been perfectly prepared to abandon loyalist Ulster if it served their war aims.

In the event, de Valera spared everyone's blushes by rejecting the British proposal as 'purely tentative', noting – perhaps mischievously – that Craigavon had been kept in the dark. But the question had potentially split the Belfast cabinet, some of whom understood the gravity of the threat posed by Germany, not just to the UK but to western civilisation in general. The question was left hanging, one of history's might-have-beens.

Winston Churchill.

The War Effort

Northern Ireland made a material contribution to the British war effort. After the crisis had passed with victory in the Battle of Britain, the German campaign in Russia and America's entry to the war, Northern Ireland's role lay in heavy industry such as shipbuilding, aircraft manufacture and military engineering, but most of all in food production. The Minister of Agriculture, Sir Basil Brooke, showed his mettle. London had asked for an increase in Northern Ireland's food production. Brooke added to the London target and promoted a vigorous campaign to increase the total tillage acreage.

He set the example by having vegetables grown on the Stormont estate and on the lawn of Queen's University. He even encouraged golf clubs to plough up their fairways for corn. The total acreage under the plough doubled during the war. One egg in every five consumed in Britain came from Northern Ireland. Cattle, sheep, milk and vegetables were shipped across to the mainland. The number of tractors in the province quadrupled. By early 1941, up to 17,000 gallons of milk crossed the Irish Sea *every day*.

More than 38,000 men and women from Northern Ireland enlisted. The official figures for fatal casualties were 2,256 for the army, 1,112 for the RAF, 843 for the Royal Navy and 524 for the merchant navy. There was one Victoria Cross, ironically won by a Catholic (volunteers from the neutral South won six). As the Battle of the Atlantic raged, the Foyle estuary at Derry became a vital naval base. But the nationalist population was never fully reconciled to the war effort and there was never any serious thought given to extending conscription to the province: it was always an incendiary subject in nationalist Ireland.

Battle of the Atlantic 1941. An RAF Blenheim Bomber and Royal Navy Destroyer attacking and destroying a German U-boat, which had targeted an Atlantic Convoy.

John Miller Andrews.

Unionist Unrest

The vigour demonstrated by Basil Brooke stood in contrast to some of his cabinet colleagues. Most had been with Craigavon from the start and were tired. Craigavon himself died suddenly in November 1940. Andrews, who replaced him, was no improvement and maintained the old guard *in situ*. Brooke was not alone in deploring what he regarded as lethargy at the top. Edmond Warnock, parliamentary secretary at the Ministry of Home Affairs, resigned in May 1940, and introduced a motion of censure the following September calling for the reconstitution of the government.

Nothing happened. Unemployment rose when it should have fallen. The government failed to attack restrictive industrial practices which weakened the war effort. Most of all, the failure to provide effective air defences was shown up for the shameful neglect it was in the devastating Luftwaffe raids of April and May 1941. Emergency evacuation plans for civilians fell short, with predicable consequences following the blitz.

In general, there was an absence of urgency at the top, only partly disguised by the efforts of industry and agriculture. It was time for a generational change. A succession of visitors and observers from

London found the Belfast government lethargic: Ernest Bevin, Minister of Labour, called it 'weak and complaisant'. Nor was there any shortage of internal critics within unionism. It all built intolerable pressure on Andrews, whose response to criticism was dilatory. Eventually, he was forced out by a rebellion of backbenchers and junior ministers. He resigned in April 1943, to be replaced by Brooke.

Rescue workers search through the rubble of Eglington Street in Belfast after a German Luftwaffe air raid, 7 May 1941. The entire city of Belfast, the Germans discovered, was defended by only seven anti-aircraft batteries. In short, Belfast was the most undefended city in the United Kingdom.

Prime Minister Brooke

Sir Basil Brooke had proved himself a vigorous, hands-on and very effective minister of agriculture who had driven the success of his sector in the war effort. He was also considered, with justice, to be bitterly anti-nationalist. He claimed to harbour no animus towards Catholics per se; not everyone believed him. But he had drive: no one denied that.

He cleaned out all the old guard, Dawson Bates and the rest of them. Only one member of Andrews' last cabinet survived to serve in Brooke's first. Harry Midgley, a left-wing Labour MP but reliably and robustly Protestant, was minister of public security. The new men showed increased vigour but they were in no way liberal: some were more virulently anti-Catholic than Brooke. A 1944 report described Brooke as being 'too advanced and too liberal', epithets not normally applied to him.

Sir Basil Brooke.

High Street and Bridge Street, Belfast, after air raids on Belfast in 1941.

His principal achievement in his first two years in office was to improve relations with London. He made the most of Northern Ireland's contribution to the war effort, conspicuously contrasting it with Dublin's neutrality. In return, he received increased Treasury grants for Northern Ireland to bring it closer to the British norm in areas such as health and housing, the latter a particularly urgent concern following the Belfast blitz. He personified a new urgency in government. He also had the kind of roguish charm that is useful in politics. He even got on well with members of the post-war Labour government and welcomed the welfare measures it introduced, despite the suspicions of many unionists, with their instinctive Tory sympathies.

Post-War Welfare

The reforms introduced by Clement Attlee's post-war Labour government created the welfare state. Most of them also applied to Northern Ireland, with London assuming the full cost. This last point was important, as it ended the so-called 'imperial contribution' that Northern Ireland had been paying to the UK Exchequer. Brooke had previously promised a post-war reconstruction plan of his own but this was now folded into the larger UK plan for a welfare state. The Beveridge Report, which laid the foundations of the National Health Service, was implemented in Northern Ireland.

There was a fear in some unionist quarters that all this would mean ever-greater control from London, with the associated danger of ever-greater scrutiny of the province's peculiar political foibles. One suggestion even proposed that Northern Ireland should apply for full dominion status to ensure greater independence, a sign of unionist anxiety about both socialism and metropolitan scrutiny. That would have required continued British subsidies, however, as Northern Ireland could not possibly have stood on its own two feet financially. It was a futile attempt to have cake and eat it.

The blitz had revealed the shocking condition of much jerry-built public housing. After the war, the minister of health and local government established the Northern Ireland Housing Trust, one of the great successes of the entire reconstruction project. It also nationalised the railway system. There were mutterings from the more Tory-inclined unionist backbenchers, but Brooke saw them off.

It was a somewhat different picture in another area of post-war reform: education.

Clement Attlee by George Harcourt, 1946.

The Education Act 1947

In December 1944, Minister of Education Lt-Col. Samuel Hall-Thompson published a White Paper that proposed to extend the Butler Education Act, which established free secondary education for all up to the school-leaving age of 15, to Northern Ireland. There followed three years of rancorous debate.

On the Catholic side, the great fear was state control and the loss of the Church's autonomous control of its own school system. Moreover, state control in practice would mean Protestant control. Increased capital grants to Catholic schools were dismissed as a bribe intended to draw them into the state-school net.

On the Protestant side, Hall-Thompson faced different but even more potent trouble. He proposed to scrap compulsory Bible instruction in state schools, diluting it to a more general non-denominational religious instruction and allowing teachers who could not teach this in good conscience to opt out. The United Education Committee of the Protestant Churches protested noisily. In a mirror image of the Catholic position, they wished to retain a full Protestant ethos in place of the diluted offering from the minister.

Eventually, Hall-Thompson got his legislation through in 1947. It had the short-term effect of expanding opportunities for Catholic children, which bled into the long-term effect of facilitating the development of a growing Catholic middle class a generation later, which would have considerable consequences. But the bitterness of Protestant opposition had highlighted yet again that popular Protestantism saw itself, and itself alone, as the people. To them, state schools should be Protestant schools. Catholics, who had their own reasons for educational independence, agreed.

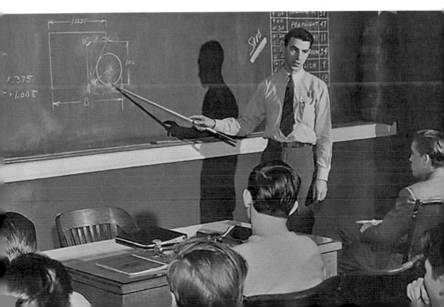

Teaching a class, late 1940s.

John A. Costello.

The Ireland Act 1949

Ever since 1937, the constitutional position of the South had been ambiguous. The constitution was formally a republican document but the state remained a British dominion and a member of the Commonwealth. In 1948, John A. Costello, briefly taoiseach following a surprise election defeat for de Valera, declared Ireland a full republic and withdrew from the Commonwealth.

Under pressure from Brooke, Attlee passed the Ireland Act, which declared 'that in no event will Northern Ireland or any part thereof cease to be part … of the United Kingdom without the consent of the parliament of Northern Ireland'. At the same time, it continued to treat citizens of the Republic the same as before and relations with Dublin stabilised.

For Northern Ireland, it was a reward for its wartime contribution, especially its key role in the Battle of the Atlantic. The contrast with southern neutrality was hard to miss. Brooke immediately called a one-issue election on the constitutional status of Northern Ireland, got the desired result and was able to trumpet to London that Ulster (as he misnamed it) was British. In Dublin, an All-Party Anti-Partition Committee had been set up to mobilise the nationalist vote in the North and to highlight the partition issue generally. It raised funds through after-Mass collections on Sunday mornings, perfect ammunition for the unionists, who called it 'the chapel gate election'. Despite the efforts of the committee Brooke won easily, wiping out the NILP as a rival Protestant force.

Brooke was now master of all he surveyed. He had his constitutional guarantee. Internal opposition was neutered and nationalists could cheerfully be ignored. Northern Ireland entered upon its brief years of Protestant paradise.

Clement Attlee.

The Anti-Partition League

The Anti-Partition League developed out of the Anti-Partition Committee that had mobilised for the 1945 general election in Northern Ireland. Formally established in 1947, its primary purpose was to deploy the only weapon it possessed: rhetoric. Two years later, in 1949, a sister organisation, the All-Party Anti-Partition Committee – commonly referred to as the Mansion House Committee – was established in Dublin. It drew the adherence of leading political figures in the Republic, normally the deeply hostile and mutually suspicious legatees of the Civil War of 1922–23.

But partition was the one issue that united all shades of nationalism, so that the Mansion House

Frank Aiken.

Committee could embrace such leading figures as John A. Costello, taoiseach; Eamon de Valera, once and future taoiseach; Seán MacBride, minister for external affairs; Frank Aiken, soon to hold that same cabinet post and a permanent member of all de Valera's cabinets since 1932; and William Norton, leader of the Labour Party.

It collected funds for the peaceful unification of Ireland, although how they were to be efficiently disbursed to that end remained something of a mystery. It promoted anti-partition propaganda, funding nationalist candidates in Northern Ireland and publishing pamphlets. It also established an anti-partition league in Britain. De Valera, now in opposition for several years, took the opportunity to tour the world to cast anathemas upon the evils of partition. The unionists simply ignored the whole thing, as usual.

THE PARTITION OF IRELAND IS A CRIME AGAINST INTERNATIONAL JUSTICE

IT MUST BE RIGHTED

ULSTER

PARTITION BOUNDARY
MAJORITY AGAINST PARTITION
25% TO 50% AGAINST PARTITION
MAJORITY FOR PARTITION

Partition label or stamp.

Northern Ireland's Post-War Economy

Although agriculture continued to be the largest single economic and commercial activity in Northern Ireland after the war, industry – especially in the Lagan Valley – continued its post-war recovery. In 1951, Harland & Wolff were either building or holding forward orders for 68 ships, including the aircraft carrier HMS *Eagle*, the largest ship in the Royal Navy. Employment was once more in excess of 20,000. But it was short-lived. German and Japanese shipyards gradually recovered from their wartime devastation; the development of long-haul passenger jet aircraft transformed international travel; and Britain's long, slow disengagement from empire had begun.

HMS *Eagle* was laid down on 24 October 1942 at Harland & Wolff shipyard in Belfast as one of four ships of the Audacious class. These were laid down during the Second World War as part of the British naval build-up during that conflict.

By 1962, the workforce at Harland & Wolff had been cut almost in half from its 1951 high. Its last big order, for the passenger ship *Canberra*, lost the company more than £1m. As with shipbuilding, so with linen, the heart of the province's textile industry. Once again, 1951 was the maximum year for employment, but the end of the Korean War in 1953 hit the market hard. In the course of the 1950s, one-third of all textile employees lost their jobs. Synthetic fibres produced cheaply in foreign markets were increasingly dominant.

Agricultural productivity increased during the decade, but agricultural employment did not, as labour-saving devices – tractors, especially – became more numerous. Overall, though, while the future looked ominous, the 1950s was a decade of increased personal prosperity for the people of the province. In due time, the decline of the older industries was compensated by a new policy of inward investment, especially from the United States.

Harland & Wolff workers.

The Flags and Emblems Act 1954

The Flags and Emblems (Display) Act (Northern Ireland), 1954 was grounded in fiction and illusion. It permitted the RUC to remove any emblem – the Irish tricolour was the most obvious target – that might cause a social disturbance. Since the tricolour was routinely flown at nationalist events, not least at sports contests held under the aegis of the Gaelic Athletic Association (GAA), that was offering a hostage to fortune. Contrariwise, it offered legal protections to public displays of the Union flag.

The Union flag was in no sense a 'national' flag but the primary badge of unionist loyalty. The nationalists felt zero loyalty to it and regarded it as the party banner of their sectarian enemy. In that sense, unionist complaints of long standing – that nationalists were an irreconcilable fifth column – had some merit. But it is hard to see how the 1954 act did anything except encourage fanatics on both sides and widen the gap between them.

The government had argued that loyal Ulster subjects should be able to display their loyalty without hindrance and be subject to all possible legal protection. It claimed that the Union flag was the national flag, which was both true and untrue. It was, claimed the government, above politics in the same way as the crown was. Each of these dubious contentions was soon to be challenged in the most unambiguous manner. When the first distant rumbles of what became the Troubles occurred ten years later, flags and emblems were predictably at the tense heart of things.

Period Irish tricolour flag.

The Ulster Banner flying over a unionist area of Derry, and the Irish tricolour flying over a nationalist area (far left) of the city.

The Ulster flag is the St George's Cross of England, with the ancient emblem of the blood-red hand of Ulster.

Community Relations

The two communities, Protestant/unionist and Catholic/ nationalist, lived separate, parallel and unequal lives. Housing was segregated by religion as well as by class and by mutual choice. Each felt safer with their own kind. In a society that was fiercely observant on both sides, theological and doctrinal differences were emphasised rather than elided. Social life, likewise, was generally segregated: there were Catholic pubs and Protestant pubs, with minimal mixing between the two. That said, there was also a necessary degree of forbearance between the two sides, provided incendiary topics were avoided, simply in order to grease the wheels of social life. This was more common in the countryside than in the towns.

A wall running the length of the Springmartin Road in Belfast is a so-called 'peace line' between the Protestant and Catholic communities. The compound at the end of the six-metre wall is a police station. Picture from 2009.

This photograph shows the reality of divided communites, with a protective 'cage' around the gardens of the houses, already separated by a high fence.

Social life was severely segregated, again by mutual choice. Marrying out – the so-called 'mixed marriage' – was regarded as a scandal on both sides and it could be a lethal threat to one party or both. Sport seldom crossed the divide. Protestants had nothing to do with the GAA, any more than Catholics had to do with rugby, hockey or cricket. Protestants still commanded the heights of commerce and the higher professions, although the expansion of Catholic education as a result of the 1947 act would soon begin to subvert that primacy.

The decade following that act is remembered – especially by Protestants – as a kind of lost Eden. The province was at peace. Protestants, for whose convenience Northern Ireland had been specifically established, were very much in charge of things. But the enemy was never far from the gate, as events were soon to prove. The siege would be permanent.

Fergal O'Hanlon was killed at the age of 20, along with Seán South, while taking part in an attack on the RUC barracks in Brookeborough, County Fermanagh, during the Border Campaign. Several other IRA members were wounded in the attack.

The IRA Border Campaign

A northern IRA ginger group called Saor Uladh (Free Ulster) forced the hand of the leadership in Dublin. In 1954, a raid on Gough Barracks in Armagh provided a haul of arms for the cause. The actual campaign took another two years to get going. From the start, it was confined to border areas, with local majority nationalist populations; Belfast and most of the area east of the Bann remained untouched throughout. It was ever after referred to as a campaign, but it was really a loosely co-ordinated series of raids, many of them carried out with clumsy inefficiency to very little effect.

On New Year's Eve 1956, a raid on the RUC barracks in the solidly Protestant town of Brookeborough, County Fermanagh – the prime minister's estate village – resulted in the deaths of two IRA men, Fergal O'Hanlon from County Monaghan just south of the border, and Seán South of Garryowen in faraway Limerick, concerning whom a famous ballad was composed.

In the Republic, de Valera returned to power for the last time in 1957 and promptly interned IRA men, choking off their supply of manpower. He had the prestige to do it: he simply could not countenance a rival to the state's own army. The campaign limped on for a few more years, eventually being called off in 1962. Twelve republicans and six RUC men had paid with their lives. It seemed as if the whole tradition of republican militancy and violence had come to a dead end. For a few more years, this illusion was sustained.

Fergal O'Hanlon's gravestone

Monument to Fergal O'Hanlon and Seán South in Moane's Cross.

Brookeborough

Terence O'Neill

Lord Brookeborough, as Sir Basil Brooke had become in 1952, finally vacated the prime minister's office in 1963. He was succeeded by another 'Big House' unionist, Captain Terence O'Neill, an old Etonian and a Guardsman.

O'Neill had been minister of finance for the previous seven years and his succession was seamless. Despite his family's deep Ulster roots on both sides – he was descended from the Chichesters and the Clandeboye O'Neills – he seemed a more remote, patrician figure than his predecessor.

From the start, he made it clear that he favoured reforms that would bring the two communities closer by encouraging economic cross-border links and by visiting Catholic institutions in Northern Ireland. Although unyielding on the constitutional issue, O'Neill caught some of the optimistic zeitgeist of the early 1960s and created a different mood music in Northern Ireland. He favoured economic planning and greater cooperation with the trade unions. He was conscious that from 1964 there was a Labour government in London, many of whose supporters were sympathetic to Irish nationalism. He also kept an eye to the NILP in his own backyard, conscious that any successes it might have would come disproportionally from disaffected working-class Protestants. O'Neill favoured regional development to reduce the economic dependence on Belfast and the Lagan Valley. He endorsed a report that had been commissioned in Brookeborough's day which recommended the building of a new town between Lurgan and Portadown, to be called Craigavon.

As finance minister, O'Neill had admired the transformation that was being effected in the Republic by the more open policies of Lemass (de Valera's successor) and the bureaucrat T. K. Whitaker. Like them, he had done much to entice inward economic investment from abroad. He regarded Altnagelvin hospital in Derry, the first post-war hospital built from scratch in the UK since the end of the war, as a model of the possible. He oversaw the building of Belfast's first motorway. Logically, it should have run south to the border, to improve transport links with Dublin, the biggest city on the island; or if not to Dublin, then to Derry, the second city of Northern Ireland. But old habits died hard: absurdly, it ran only to the modest market town of Dungannon deep in County Tyrone. There was to be no motorway to Catholic places.

The decision to establish a second university, to be called the University of Ulster, in the Protestant town of Coleraine rather than in Derry, where there was already a university college, was especially controversial. The decision was based on the Lockwood Report, which favoured Coleraine because of its potential for expansion, something denied of the Derry site. Nonetheless, it looked bad: even if Lockwood had clean hands, the unionists who implemented his recommendation had not. O'Neill's reforming bona fides suffered accordingly.

O'Neill–Lemass, 1965

Seán Lemass was taoiseach from 1959 to 1966. His strong right arm was the brilliant T. K. Whitaker, secretary of the department of finance. Between them, they transformed the Republic, abandoning economic self-sufficiency and surfing the wave of post-war capitalist prosperity. Lemass was a pragmatist who wanted more cordial relations with Belfast. Brookeborough had snubbed him initially but O'Neill went so far as to invite Lemass to Stormont, an invitation that Lemass readily accepted. O'Neill did not inform his cabinet prior to issuing the invitation.

Lemass travelled north in January 1965 and the two men got on well, if a little tentatively at first. The meeting had an immediate effect. Nationalist leader Eddie McAteer announced that his party would assume the role of official parliamentary opposition at Stormont for the first time. In time, O'Neill made a reciprocal visit to Dublin. Neither premier was going to yield on their basic constitutional positions: they were, however,

Seán Lemass.

pragmatic realists trying to establish a good-neighbour policy. For O'Neill, this meant maintaining a high wall on partition; for Lemass, it meant economic development in the Republic such as unionists might come to envy.

But their realism came to nothing. As Lemass drove into Stormont that January midday, word of his arrival had got out. A small group of Protestant ultras, led by a figure of whom more and more was being heard, the Rev. Ian Paisley, demonstrated their devotion to the principles of the Reformation by throwing snowballs at Lemass's car. Tragically, Paisley represented a kind of future; the realists did not.

Thomas Whitaker was an Irish economist and civil servant. He was governor of the Central Bank of Ireland from 1969 to 1976 and a senator from 1977 to 1982. He is credited with a crucial role in Ireland's economic development.

Gestures Towards Nationalists

Terence O'Neill.

Pope John XXIII.

In June 1963, Pope John XXIII died in Rome. Contrary to all precedent, Terence O'Neill, newly installed as prime minister of Northern Ireland, sent a message of sympathy to William Cardinal Conway of Armagh, the head of the Catholic Church in Ireland. In his message of condolence, he was generous in his praise of the late pontiff. He specified that this message of sympathy came from the government of the province and was extended, through the cardinal, to the entire Catholic community.

O'Neill made a point of visiting Catholic institutions such as schools and even a convent. Conor Cruise O'Brien imagined the slightly bored, patrician O'Neill saying to the nuns, 'Must be very tiring for you, with all those rosary beads to tell and so on'. But the joke contained a barb: to tell beads is a pure Anglican usage, unknown to Roman Catholics. It echoed things that O'Neill, for all his well-meaning decency, actually said: 'It is frightfully hard to explain to Protestants that if you give Roman Catholics a good job and a good house … they will refuse to have 18 children, but if a Roman Catholic is jobless, and lives in the most ghastly hovel, he will rear 18 children on national assistance.'

O'Neill knew that you cannot forever disregard more than one-third of a population, especially when that segment was furnishing half of all secondary schoolchildren. But the tone was all wrong – and he represented what passed for liberalism and accommodation in his political tradition.

Captain Terence O'Neill, prime minister of Northern Ireland, shown campaigning with his wife, during a general election campaign. He was opposed in his Bannside, County Antrim, constituency by, amongst others, the Rev. Ian Paisley

The New Catholic Middle Class

Back in 1947, when Hall-Thompson had been forcing his Education Act through Stormont, much of the unionist opposition to it was grounded in a belief that if you educate Catholics, they will produce community leaders and that the union was safer if as few of them as possible got an education. It was odious but, like a lot of reactionary pessimism, prescient.

Ruairí Ó Brádaigh, President, Republican Sinn Féin, at a 1920s IRA memorial at Shankill graveyard, County Roscommon, 1994.

By the mid-1960s, the effects of the act were being felt. Fifty per cent of the school-going population required teachers and the number of Catholic teachers had expanded accordingly. Queen's University, Belfast was still substantially Protestant in its student body but the number of Catholic undergraduates was growing, not to mention those studying in universities in the Republic.

Ruairí Ó Brádaigh in 2004.

Teachers were critical. They had always had a leadership role in nationalist society. Ruairí Ó Brádaigh, soon to be the leader of Sinn Féin, was a teacher. Even more significantly, so was John Hume from Derry, shortly to be the most substantial political figure in nationalist politics. They were graduates, with all the self-possession and self-confidence that a university degree can grant. Over time, a commercial Catholic bourgeoisie would also emerge, likewise lawyers and medical practitioners in growing numbers. For the moment, it was the teachers who were most visible. It was the most important social and generational change of the day; its effects were seismic.

John Hume, from a set of paintings on a Bogside mural.

The Campaign for Social Justice

Conn McCluskey was not a teacher. He was a medical doctor based in Dungannon, at the end of the motorway. In 1964, he helped his wife Patricia to found the Campaign for Social Justice (CSJ), which evolved out of an earlier pressure group that had complained of discrimination in the allocation of local housing. Although the town was evenly split between the denominations, the customary adroit gerrymandering ensured a unionist majority on the council, which it deployed to house its own. No Catholic family had been allocated a new council house in Dungannon since 1940.

The CSJ was significant in three respects. First, its initial membership comprised only professional, educated

Conn and Patricia McCluskey.

people, a telling detail (it was founded in the house of a surgeon). Moreover, although nominally non-sectarian, the members were all Catholics. Second, it wearied of the traditional nationalist mantras, regarding the Nationalist Party as ineffective, albeit many of the CSJ's concerns were those traditionally expressed by nationalists. Third, they appealed not to Irish nationalist desire, with its fixation on partition, but to British fair play. This was the seed corn from which would emerge the civil rights movement.

It accused unionism of overt discrimination against the west of the province and against Catholics generally. In August 1968, following a particularly brazen housing allocation to a 19-year-old single Protestant woman, her intended house was occupied by Austin Currie, the local nationalist MP. He was evicted by an RUC man who just happened to be the woman's brother. There followed a protest march of 2,500 people from Coalisland to Dungannon to highlight this shocking example of unionist local government practice. It was the spark that ignited a long fuse.

Austin Currie was Northern Ireland MP for East Tyrone, 1964–72. He later served in the short-lived power-sharing executive and was a NI Assembly member in the 1980s, before moving to the Republic, where he ran for president without success in 1991.

The Campaign for Democracy in Ulster

The British general election of 1964 brought Labour to power for the first time in 13 years. Harold Wilson's backbenches contained a significant number of MPs who were troubled by the peculiar political arrangements in Northern Ireland, especially in local government. Wilson was reluctant to get involved in Irish affairs – the default setting for all governments since the 1920s – but neither could he ignore influential backbenchers. In June 1965, a group of these formed themselves into the Campaign for Democracy in Ulster (CDU).

British Prime Minister Harold Wilson, in 1964.

It pressed for a full enquiry into allegations of discrimination on religious grounds; called for electoral law to align fully with the rest of the UK; and campaigned for the full application of the Race Relations Act to Northern Ireland. It emphasised that the border was not the issue – this demonstrated the influence of McCluskey's CSJ – but that the full application of British rights in British territory was.

The CDU was more a straw in the wind than an obviously successful campaigning group. It kept the question of Northern Ireland alive on government backbenches in the House of Commons. Its attempts at raising specific issues concerning policy were met with the usual stonewall answer, that under the Government of Ireland Act 1920 such matters were within the competence of Stormont and should not therefore be raised at Westminster. This, as events were soon to prove, was no more than a convenient excuse. The CDU had the support of up to 100 Labour MPs at different times, but one was more important than most. In 1966 Gerry Fitt became MP for West Belfast.

Gerry Fitt, republican MP for West Belfast, on a visit to the Home Office in London in 1970 to complain about the army's behaviour in the Roman Catholic Falls Road area of Belfast.

Gerry Fitt

Fitt was a former merchant navy sailor who had been on Belfast City Council for a few years before winning West Belfast. He made an immediate impact on Westminster: fast-talking, chain-smoking, he spoke in plain but colourful language that appealed to many Labour MPs. He organised trips to the province for curious MPs, for whom Northern Ireland up close was a revelation.

Gerry Fitt, ennobled as Lord Fitt, founder of the SLDP and MP for West Belfast, with his mother, early 1980s.

Like most British people, even well-disposed Labour MPs were woefully ignorant of Ulster realities, so Fitt's tutorials were an important exercise in consciousness raising.

Although he was to go on to be leader of the future SDLP and – briefly – deputy chief executive of the short-lived Northern Ireland Executive in 1974, Fitt was a political maverick and a loner. He was self-educated: at sea, he had read widely in politics and law but never lost the common touch. He was a good platform speaker and a natural populist, with a wisecracking wit that people related to.

He won his battle honours with the civil rights movement in Derry in 1968, when the RUC baton-charged a march. Fitt received facial wounds: the sight of a Westminster MP being batoned into a bloody mess on a British street was broadcast globally thanks to the presence of television cameras. The world became aware of this peculiar place, described in one London newspaper headline as 'John Bull's Political Slum'.

Thousands of people lined the streets of Derry to march for equality and to mark the 50th anniversary of the 5 October 1968 civil rights march from Duke Street in Derry.

NICRA

The Wolfe Tone Society, Muintir Wolfe Tone, evolved from IRA organisations set up in 1963 to mark the bicentenary of the 1763 birth of Wolfe Tone. Wolfe Tone was a leading Irish revolutionary figure and is regarded as the father of Irish republicanism.

The Northern Ireland Civil Rights Association (NICRA) was a conscious echo of the civil rights movement in the United States. Its aims were similar to those of the CSJ, from which it evolved. Its basic demands were for one man [sic] one vote in local elections, thus ending the property qualification that favoured unionists; an end to gerrymandering; fair allocation of public housing; and repeal of the Special Powers Act and the disbandment of the B Specials. It also sought mechanisms for investigating and dealing with complaints of unfair practices in public administration. Once again, partition was not the issue. It was a programme to harmonise Northern Ireland with the rest of the United Kingdom.

From the start, however, it had republican elements. Its first executive committee contained two members of the Wolfe Tone Society and a Republican Labour Stormont MP. The Wolfe

Tone Society was a ginger group that reflected the republican movement's swerve to the left, partly under the influence of the 1960s' zeitgeist and partly as a corrective to the shambles of the border campaign.

Although the early NICRA valiantly embraced people from all political persuasions – it even had a member of the Young Unionists on its first committee – it was, inevitably, preponderantly nationalist in tone. The presence of republicans gave unionists a perfect excuse to smear it as an IRA front, and it was true that the Wolfe Tone Society had adopted a determined 'entryist' policy.

NICRA organised protest marches to highlight the issues that concerned it. Following the Dungannon march of August 1968, it was resolved that the next protest would be held in Derry in October.

Civil rights poster.

Northern Ireland Civil Rights
ASSOCIATION

A CIVIL RIGHTS MARCH

WILL BE HELD IN **DERRY** ON SATURDAY, 5TH OCT.

COMMENCING AT 3-30 p.m.

ASSEMBLY POINT : WATERSIDE RAILWAY STATION
MARCH TO THE DIAMOND
Where a PUBLIC METTING will take place

Derry, 1968

There had been no television cameras at Dungannon but there were in Derry on 5 October. A crew from RTÉ in Dublin had come up to cover the NICRA march. It had been banned by the Stormont Minister of Home Affairs, William Craig, but the organisers ignored the ban and went ahead anyway. This was done with some reluctance: moderates such as the McCluskeys were persuaded by radicals such as Eamonn McCann of the Derry Housing Action Committee, who made no bones about inviting a police over-reaction.

They got an over-reaction that changed the face of Northern Ireland for ever. About 400 people assembled at the railway station, located on the mainly Protestant Waterside (east bank) of the Foyle. They set off and soon emerged onto nearby Duke Street, still on the Waterside, there to be met by the RUC. What followed was little short of a police riot. Seventy-seven marchers were injured, including the bloodied Gerry Fitt, and Eddie McAteer, the leader of the Nationalist Party. Eleven RUC men also received injuries.

A subsequent British government report found that the batoning of marchers by police was unjustifiable, although acknowledging that some marchers – including Fitt – had behaved irresponsibly.

Such qualifications hardly mattered: the television cameras had done their work. John Bull's political slum was on screens and front pages, where it would remain for a generation. For the first time since partition, unionism was seriously on the back foot. It had to explain and justify its peculiar institutions to an increasingly perplexed and sceptical world opinion.

RUC policemen during a civil rights demonstration in Derry city on 5 October 1968. From an RTÉ photograph.

Ian Paisley

For every action, there is a reaction. Even the tentative, modest change of tone represented by Terence O'Neill was sufficient to alarm loyalist ultras who deplored any departure from traditional no-surrender unionism. This element found its stentorian voice in the person of Rev. Ian Paisley, founder and head of the Free Presbyterian Church.

Although his formal following was small at first, his uncompromising sectarianism touched a silent nerve in the Protestant community. Paisley was loudly unapologetic and wonderfully charismatic.

He led the opposition to the original NICRA march at Dungannon but it passed off without incident. After Derry, however, everything was transformed. The next major NICRA protest was scheduled for Armagh on 30 November. Paisley and his followers mustered in numbers in the small city centre and took it over. For this, Paisley and his chief sidekick, Major Ronald Bunting, were sentenced to three months' imprisonment for unlawful assembly.

It was the making of Paisley, investing him with the mantle of martyrdom. He went on to transform unionism from within, founding and leading the Democratic Unionist Party (DUP) which eventually displaced mainstream unionism as the principal voice of Protestant opinion. He was elected first to Stormont, then to Westminster; he was at the heart of every mischief that followed on the Protestant side of things, until in old age he softened somewhat and ended up as first minister of Northern Ireland. It was an operatic career.

November Reforms

Brian Faulkner, Baron Faulkner of Downpatrick, was the sixth and last prime minister of Northern Ireland, from March 1971 until his resignation a year later.

On 4 November Terence O'Neill, William Craig and Brian Faulkner, the minister of commerce and an ambitious rising star in the unionist firmament, were summoned to meet Harold Wilson in London. Wilson was under pressure from members of the CDU on his own backbenches to hang tough. While renewing the pledge contained in the 1949 Ireland Act – no transfer of territory to the Republic without the consent of Stormont – he also bluntly threatened the withdrawal of financial support unless Belfast got its house in order.

Chastened, O'Neill's cabinet produced a five-point programme. Local authority housing allocation was to be reformed by employing a points system. An ombudsman would be in place to adjudicate on citizens' complaints. Londonderry Corporation was to be abolished and replaced by a development commission. The Special Powers Act would be repealed when it was judged safe to do so (it was not so judged until 1970 and then only under pressure from London). Finally, there was a move, but only a move, towards one man, one vote in local authority elections; the company vote was to be abolished but only ratepayers were granted the franchise for the moment.

All this was unquestionably a victory for nationalists, who had achieved more reforms in a couple of months than they had in a lifetime. Likewise, it alarmed many on the unionist side, for in zero-sum Ulster a win for one side meant a loss for the other. Still, for the moment, it appeared to do the trick. The tensions eased without disappearing. Grumbles on the unionist side, not least in the cabinet from hardliners like William Craig, were muted. The province held its breath.

Ulster Vanguard leader William Craig addressing workers from James Mackie and Sons in 1972. They had marched from their Springfield Road factory to the City Hall in protest against the lack of security that allowed IRA gunmen to shoot at and injure their fellow workers leaving the factory in Belfast.

Crossroads

At this delicate moment, Terence O'Neill took a gamble. He looked past the critics in his cabinet such as Craig and appealed directly to the people of Northern Ireland. He went on radio and television to state: 'Ulster stands at the crossroads. I believe you know me well enough by now to appreciate that I am not a man given to extravagant language. But ... our conduct over the coming days and weeks will decide our future.... For more than five years now I have tried to heal some of the deep divisions in our community. I did so because I could not see how an Ulster divided against itself could hope to stand. I made it clear that a Northern Ireland based upon the interests of any one section rather than upon the interests of all could have no long-term future.'

The speech was well received on both sides of the border, not least by the leaders of mainstream northern nationalism. In the short term, it worked: O'Neill received overwhelming media support and a substantial vote of confidence from his MPs. He even felt strong enough to dismiss William Craig.

It was not just that events, driven on by radicals, conspired against him. It was that there was an evasion at the heart of the crossroads speech. Northern Ireland existed solely to advance and protect 'the interests of one section', the Protestant community. Whatever tentative accommodations have been made between the two sides in the subsequent half century – and these have been fragile – in 1968 there was no chance of such a historic rapprochement happening.

Northern Ireland Prime Minister Terence O'Neill (left) and An Taoiseach Jack Lynch pose for photographs after their meeting in Dublin in January 1968. This shot was taken for RTÉ Television News.

Burntollet

The People's Democracy was a small but influential left-wing group formed in Queen's University. They were under the influence of the recent protests in Paris, the earlier Selma-Montgomery march in the United States and the radical temper of the late 1960s generally.

Against the advice of the mainstream NICRA leaders, they set out on a march from Belfast to Derry to protest against police brutality and continuing inequalities in Northern Irish life. Originally not many more than 40, they gathered sympathisers along the way and their numbers had grown to some hundreds by the time they reached Burntollet Bridge on the approach to Derry. There, a gang of about 200 loyalists laid a well-prepared ambush for the march. They were helped by off-duty B Specials and the marchers received little protection from the 80 RUC men accompanying them. Bricks, bottles, iron bars and other offensive weapons were deployed with malevolent abandon.

The earliest part of the march stumbled on into Derry, having got past the ambush site before the main attack began. When the rest, battered and bleeding, eventually followed, they found their way to the Bogside, the Catholic area beyond the city walls. There followed days of civil disturbance, not helped by clumsy and partisan policing by the RUC.

The marchers, in their youthful naivety, imagined that they were part of an international movement – first Alabama, then Paris, now Northern Ireland – in which working-class solidarity would overcome evil. There was no such solidarity: those who attacked the marchers at Burntollet were working class and desired no solidarity with their Catholic confrères. Burntollet opened an older, more local, can of worms.

Commemoration march poster from 1979.

TENTH COMMEMORATION MARCH 1969-1979

March Leaves Toome Friday Jan.5th. Mass Rally At Burntollet Bridge Sunday Jan.7th.

A PEOPLE UNDEFEATED

Issued by the Burntollet Commemoration Committee

BURNTOLLET

The General Election, 1969

O'Neill called a Northern Ireland general election for 24 February 1969. The result was confusion, as the monolithic nature of local politics crumbled under the pressure of events. Brian Faulkner had already resigned from the cabinet over O'Neill's decision to establish the Cameron Commission to examine the causes of the recent disturbances. The Unionist Party split in all sorts of confusing ways, but the basic split was between those who supported O'Neill's modest reforms and those who opposed them. On the nationalist side, independents, members of People's Democracy (PD), republicans and socialists crowded the ballot papers along with the traditional Nationalist Party.

The result was a pyrrhic victory for O'Neill. Of the 39 unionists returned, 27 supported the prime minister. Ten were opposed to him and a further two dithered.

In a development of equal significance on the nationalist side, independents associated with the civil rights campaign displaced some Nationalist Party members. This happened most tellingly in the Foyle constituency of Derry, where John Hume – a local teacher, civil rights activist and leading figure in the credit union movement – ousted Eddie McAteer, the Nationalist Party leader.

O'Neill claimed victory but must have known that he was fatally weakened. In his mainstream unionist movement a significant minority opposed him outright. In his Bannside constituency, his margin over Ian Paisley was embarrassingly small: 1,414 out of a total poll of 16,386 on a turnout of 78.7 per cent. He did not even win a majority of votes cast, the remainder going to Michael Farrell (PD), who hoovered up the minority Catholic vote.

Rev. Ian Paisley is accompanied by his wife in a procession through Lisburn, County Antrim, to launch his 1969 general election campaign.

Bernadette Devlin

Bernadette Devlin was a 22-year-old final-year psychology student at Queen's University when she rose to prominence in the People's Democracy movement. She was in Duke Street, Derry, on 5 October 1968, and at Burntollet at the turn of the year. She was dazzlingly eloquent and in March 1969 she was elected to Westminster, where her maiden speech electrified the House of Commons.

That August, she was a central figure in the Battle of the Bogside, in which she encouraged Catholic resistance to the police and to Protestant mobs. She caught the world's attention and was variously compared to Dolores Ibárruri (La Pasionaria) and Joan of Arc. In December, she was convicted of incitement to riot, obstruction and disorderly behaviour and given a six-month prison sentence. Once released and back in the Commons, she punched Home Secretary Reginald Maudling, having accused him of lying about the events of Bloody Sunday.

She lost her seat in 1974 and thereafter faded from prominence, although she was still a visible figure in Northern Ireland life. She moved ever further towards the militant republican fringes, supporting the Maze Prison hunger strikers. In 1981, she and her husband nearly died in an attack on their home by loyalist thugs. In 1994, she helped to carry the coffin of Dominic McGlinchey, a notorious republican gunman whom she praised in glowing terms. But it was the early months and years at the start of the Troubles that made her name and gave her place in history.

Bernadette Devlin delivering a speech.

James Chichester-Clark

On 21 April 1969, a series of attacks on the Silent Valley reservoir threatened Belfast's water supply. It was believed to have been the work of the IRA but it was actually that of the Ulster Volunteer Force (UVF), a loyalist paramilitary gang. It weakened Terence O'Neill even further. Two days later, his government announced the concession of one man, one vote in local government, prompting his minister of agriculture, Major James Chichester-Clark, to resign. Chichester-Clark said that he objected to the timing of the concession, not to the principle.

A week later, Chichester-Clark was prime minister. O'Neill resigned, realising that his political position was hopeless. Chichester-Clark ordered an amnesty for prisoners convicted of political offences and appealed for calm. But the situation was spinning out of control. The terrible events of August 1969 in Derry and Belfast saw

James Chichester-Clark.

the deployment of the British Army and the summoning of Chichester-Clark to London, where he was effectively instructed to disband the B Specials and disarm the RUC. A new chief constable, Sir Arthur Young, was sent from England to head the police.

Chichester-Clark was now trapped between a London government pressing for reforms and a mutinous loyalist support base that was prepared to resist such measures, by force if necessary. He lasted until March 1971, at which point he threw in the towel and was succeeded by Brian Faulkner. Thus a representative of the mercantile middle class replaced the last of the 'big house' unionists.

The poster refers to Major Chichester-Clark, prime minister of Northern Ireland from May 1969 to March 1971. The juggling is suggestive of Chichester-Clark using sectarian division to maintain control of both Protestants and Catholics in Northern Ireland.

First Deaths

On the night of 13 July 1969, Francis McCloskey, a 67-year-old man from Dungiven, County Derry, was found lying by the roadside. He had been struck by a police baton. He died the next day. Two days later, on 16 July, a 42-year-old taxi driver from Derry, Samuel Devenney, died from injuries he had sustained in a police beating in April. The circumstances were opaque: there had been rioting in the Bogside and the RUC, while pursuing rioters, burst into Devenney's house, although it is unclear what part, if any, Devenney had played in the disturbances. At any rate, he suffered internal injuries and had a heart attack.

The new chief constable of the RUC, Sir Arthur Young, accused his own force of a cover-up, stating in November 1970 that there had been a conspiracy of silence among members of the force in order to conceal the identity of those involved in the attack on Devenney. Incidents like this reverberated in London, where Wilson's government determined on reform

Samuel Devenney, a Catholic father of nine, was killed when several RUC officers broke into his house and, in a fit of unprovoked violence, beat several members of his family and fatally injured him.

of the security forces, especially in response to the dramatic escalation of violence that followed in August in Derry and Belfast.

McCloskey and Devenney were the first victims of the Troubles. More than 3,000 people would follow them as a direct result of the violence that lasted for the next 30 years. Of these, more than 2,000 were civilians, although that number includes paramilitaries on both sides.

Poster produced by People's Democracy, probably referencing the dismantling of barricades in Belfast during 1969.

Sir Arthur Edwin Young,
by Walter Bird, 1965.

Derry & Belfast, 1969

Riots in August 1969 culminated in the Battle of the Bogside, involving a huge nationalist communal uprising in Derry. The riot started in a confrontation between Catholic residents of the Bogside, police, and members of the Apprentice Boys of Derry who were due to march past the Bogside.

The Apprentice Boys of Derry are an Orange fraternity. Their name recalls the 13 young apprentices who shut the gates of the city against the troops of King James II in 1689.

In August 1969, Derry was a tinder box. The memory of the police battles following Burntollet was still fresh and the largely nationalist population faced the Orange marching season – the summer months – with apprehension. For loyalists, however,

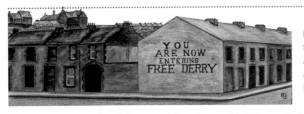

Free Derry Corner in the Bogside, part of the autonomous nationalist area of Free Derry in Northern Ireland between 1969 and 1972.

Derry was sacred soil because the siege of 1689 was baked into their historical memory.

The Apprentice Boys' march took place on 12 August. Already that summer, there had been riots in Derry and Belfast. Now, the Apprentice Boys marched around the walls of Derry as if marking out territory. At the edge of the Bogside, missiles were thrown at them and in no time a full-scale riot was in progress. This time the Bogsiders were prepared: food supplies were laid in; Molotov cocktails were available. The Battle of the Bogside lasted for 50 hours and set the people against the police and the B Specials. The people won: exhausted, the security forces withdrew. Then Belfast exploded. On 14 August, Protestant mobs – incensed by what they saw as a Catholic victory in Derry – attacked Catholic areas. Hundreds of houses were burned out; thousands of people were left homeless or forced to move. Six people, including a nine-year-old boy, were killed.

What also died was any hope of reconciliation. This was naked sectarian street warfare in a dysfunctional state. The optimism that had attended O'Neill's pallid reforms evaporated.

Jack Lynch's Broadcast

The appalling events in Northern Ireland had repercussions in the Republic. The Fianna Fáil government under Jack Lynch contained hard-line republicans and the party generally was emotionally and rhetorically republican. Lynch was a temperate man, as were many of his senior colleagues, but the pressure from hardliners, both in the cabinet and in the party generally, was real.

An Taoiseach Jack Lynch, June 1968.

Lynch went on television to announce that army field hospitals would be set up near the border to help those injured in the rioting. He added: 'It is clear now that the present situation cannot be allowed to continue. It is evident that the Stormont government is no longer in control of the situation. Indeed the present situation is the inevitable outcome of the policies pursued for decades by successive Stormont governments. It is clear that the Irish government can no longer stand by and see innocent people injured and perhaps worse.'

That last phrase was frequently misquoted by hotheads as 'cannot stand idly by', but what did it mean? What could Dublin do? Republicans hoped that it meant direct intervention in the North, but how? Its army would not have got above Newry, if even that far. Likewise, loyalists believed that this was a declaration of war. It was not: it was the least Lynch could do, in an impossible situation, to appease the hardliners in his own party. For the moment, it worked. But it also indicated, not for the first time, that at the heart of nationalist ambition there was a terrible impotence, tempered only by rhetoric.

Jack Lynch in an RTÉ studio in September/October 1972. Lynch served as a Fianna Fáil TD, minister for education, minister for industry and commerce and minister for finance before becoming taoiseach in 1966.

The British Army Arrives

The only force remotely capable of separating the two sides was the British Army. On 14 August 1969, the Stormont government asked for troops to be deployed and London agreed. Later that day, a company of the Prince of Wales's Own Regiment arrived in Derry. At first, it received a welcome from the Bogsiders and other beleaguered Catholics but that wasn't expected to last – and it didn't. James Callaghan, the home secretary, assured the House of Commons that 'this is a limited operation' and that the troops would be withdrawn when law and order was restored. They weren't because it wasn't.

The arrival of the army inevitably meant growing political involvement from London. James Callaghan was the cabinet member with direct responsibility. He confided to a colleague that he thought that there was no prospect of a solution. There was talk of abolishing Stormont and reverting to direct rule from London but the cabinet was split on the issue; the old instinct to keep Northern Ireland at arm's length died hard. It was one of the great might-have-beens of the whole conflict. By the time it was eventually forced on London, three years later, it was too late. By then, relations between nationalists and the army had soured. This enabled hardline republicans to represent the army as a mere tool of the hated Stormont regime. It did not take much to persuade nationalists that the British Army was anything other than an alien force, albeit one that had done some good in the short term. In the long term, it was being asked to act as a police auxiliary, a job for which no army has either the training or the stomach.

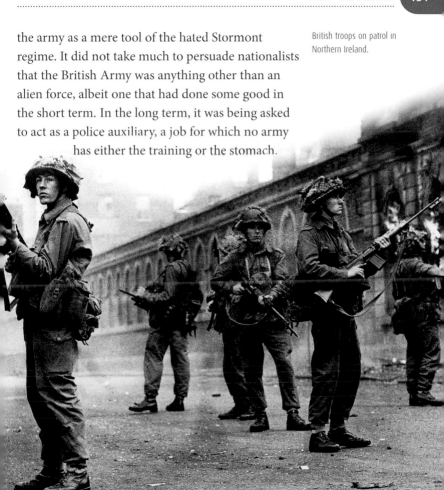

British troops on patrol in Northern Ireland.

The First IRA Casualty

Gerald McAuley.

After the fiasco of the 1956–62 Border Campaign, the IRA and republicanism generally had sought an alternative course. Under the influence of a left-wing Dublin leadership, it had embraced socialist policies and the politics of social protest. None of this was much use to Belfast nationalists when loyalist mobs burned and wrecked their streets in mid-August 1969. The IRA began to come back to life, not on pure ideological or republican grounds, but as a simple matter of terrible necessity: the imperative for communal defence against a murderous sectarian enemy.

In the Clonard area of working-class West Belfast, Billy McKee, an IRA activist, formed an ad hoc Clonard Defence Committee to try to mitigate the effects of the loyalist assault. That assault was taking full advantage of the IRA's absence. Whatever its larger ambitions for Irish unity, the Belfast IRA was first and last a community defence militia, there precisely to do what it had up to now conspicuously failed to do. The fact that the RUC and the B Specials were not exactly restraining loyalist gangs made the point even more eloquently.

McKee managed to get his hands on a few guns. Bombay Street, off the Falls Road, in the heart of republican Belfast, was ablaze from end to end. Gerald McAuley, a young volunteer with Fianna Éireann, the IRA's youth wing, was helping to move people from Bombay Street, when he was shot dead by a loyalist sniper on nearby Waterville Street. He was the first member of the IRA to die in the Troubles. He was 15 years old.

Troops in Bombay Street in a photograph from the Belfast Archive project.

IN MEMORY OF
Fian GERALD McAULEY (AGED 15)
KILLED WHILE DEFENDING
THE PEOPLE OF CLONARD
ON THE 15th AUGUST 1969

ERECTED BY THE GREATER CLONARD EX-PRISONERS
ASSOCIATION

Memorial to Gerald McAuley.

James Callaghan Arrives

Home Secretary James Callaghan visited the province twice in six weeks. He urged even more reforms on Chichester-Clark, including a reconstruction of the RUC, to be superintended by a committee under Lord Hunt, a former British Army officer. Hunt's report, which sparked violent protests from loyalists, recommended the disarming of the RUC and the replacement of the B Specials by a new reserve force under army control.

A tribunal was established under an English judge, Lord Scarman, to examine the causes of the recent violence. Callaghan also got commitments of further administrative reform from the Stormont government. There would be a central housing authority to tackle one of the worst social injustices.

Callaghan was a heavyweight, the only person to have occupied all the so-called great offices of state: chancellor of the exchequer; home secretary; foreign secretary; prime minister. His mere presence in Northern Ireland was evidence that the hands-off policy, pursued so assiduously by London since partition, was no longer sustainable.

James Callaghan and James Chichester-Clark.

The reforms he urged on Stormont – he might with justice be said to have bullied them – enraged hardline loyalists and drew forth the predictable response. In October 1969 there were two nights of rioting on the Shankill Road in the heart of loyalist West Belfast, and the first police death. Constable Victor Arbuckle of the RUC was shot dead, probably by the UVF (it wasn't just the IRA that had sprung back to life). He was 29 years of age.

Soldiers of the British Army seek cover after shots were fired in the Shankill Road, Belfast. Earlier that day RUC Constable Victor Arbuckle had been shot dead by Loyalists during street disturbances.

The Cameron Report

Following the initial outbreak of violence in Derry in October 1968, the Northern Ireland government set up a three-man commission to examine the circumstances that led to the disturbances. It was chaired by Lord Cameron, a Scottish judge. The decision to set up the commission precipitated the resignation of Brian Faulkner as minister of commerce. The Cameron Commission reported in September 1969.

It criticised successive Stormont governments and identified seven principal causes of the violence: a nationalist sense of injustice, especially concerning housing allocation; sectarian discrimination in some local government appointments; gerrymandering; the sectarian nature of the B Specials; resentment at the Special Powers Act; Protestant fears of rising Catholic numbers; and the lethargic response of the Belfast authorities to all or some of these grievances.

The commission also deplored the activities of loyalist extremists and was critical of the RUC, whose days as the unreformed force of yore were now clearly numbered. It made the point that NICRA's original list of grievances was sustained by the very fact that reforms had already been effected to address some of them, which would hardly have happened had the complaints been groundless or otherwise capable of being ignored in the traditional manner. It was critical of republican and radical elements that used NICRA to raise the temperature, but in general its report focused on the shortcomings of the entire government, administrative and police structure. As such, it was the first dispassionate official examination of Britain's 'political slum'. Psychologically, Northern Ireland would never be quite the same again.

A photograph by John White, who was born in the the Ballymacarret, Short Strand district in 1930. Before his death in 1992, he captured the dramatic changes in this small industrial enclave of Belfast.

The Hunt Report

The rioting on the Shankill Road that took the life of RUC Constable Victor Arbuckle was triggered by the publication of the Hunt Report. It recommended a radical re-fix in policing and security arrangements in Northern Ireland. Unsurprisingly, this caused genuine alarm among Protestants, who had long come to think of the security forces as their shield against republican insurgency.

The report called for the disarming of the RUC and the replacement of the B Specials with an army reserve force that ultimately became the Ulster Defence Regiment (UDR). Just as the Hunt Report alarmed Protestant opinion, it delighted those on the other side who felt that the NICRA campaign had been thoroughly vindicated. But Northern Ireland had always been a zero-sum society. A gain for one side was inevitably regarded as an absolute loss for the other.

One immediate result of the report was the appointment of the first 'outsider' as the new chief constable of the RUC. On 10 October, barely a month after the Cameron and Hunt Reports,

Contemporary Ógra Shinn Féin sticker regarding the RUC.

Sir Arthur Young of the City of London Police was appointed. The choice was either made by or directly approved by Harold Wilson. Young talked about creating an inclusive force to serve all the community; loyalists immediately interpreted this as liberal metropolitan guff that meant going soft on republicans.

In other reforms, a ministry of community relations was established, as was an independent commissioner for complaints.

Flax Street and Crumlin Road, North Belfast. In August and September 1969, Loyalist attacks on the nationalist areas of Belfast sparked deadly communal rioting. Fearful of fresh attacks, Catholics formed local defence committees and erected barricades.

Fair Employment Issue

Because of the three tragic decades of the Troubles, it is easy to overlook the quickened pace of reform in late 1969. Violence had done its work. London had woken up to the 'peculiar institutions' and practices in Northern Ireland and had leant heavily on the Belfast government to move at a pace of change that would have been impossible to contemplate had Stormont been left to itself.

The question of fair employment was not easily or quickly fixed. In the public service, whose top echelons were almost wholly Protestant, new protocols were established that aimed to eliminate, or at least mitigate, the worst cases of discrimination. That in turn meant potentially turning a blind eye to Protestant educational advantage – still a reality – by awarding positions or promotion to candidates who may not have been the best qualified.

In the private sector, the government's ability to intervene was less obvious. Geographical location of businesses, informal networks based on sports clubs and suchlike, and availability of relevant skills that might be more easily found in one community than another all fed this problem. What no one could have anticipated is what actually happened: that the rising number of Catholic graduates would lead to a greater nationalist presence in professional and commercial life, until, in some areas, it dominated it.

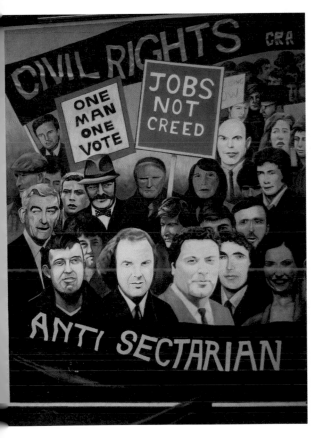

The 1968 civil rights mural showing SDLP's John Hume and Ivan Cooper in the nationalist Catholic Bogside area of Derry, also known as Free Derry. It is one of 12 murals painted from 1993 to 2008 by three local artists who called themselves the ogside Artists.

Community Relations & Complaints

The two most obvious institutional reforms of 1969 were the establishment of the ministry of community relations and the independent commissioner for complaints. The new department was charged with overseeing the structural and institutional reforms in the public sector. Its mere presence introduced a new ethic in the province's public life, one that endured.

The commissioner for complaints was in effect an ombudsman. His principal role was to examine and adjudicate upon complaints of discrimination or biased administration.

Both of these reforms are now almost wholly forgotten in the welter of violence and tragedy that enveloped Northern Ireland. But they worked to a degree that might have surprised their sponsors. It was inevitably a slow process rather than a quick fix, but between them these institutions and their successors changed mentalities in Northern Ireland.

It is commonplace to note that, quite early in the Troubles, most of the demands of the NICRA had either been met or were on their way to being met. But unionists had a point when they said it was all just a blind for a republican resurgence and that unionism should not yield an inch. That was impossible, but they were not wrong about the centrality of the national question, as was soon demonstrated.

Local Election Reform

Of all the reforms made in the autumn of 1969, none was more symbolic than the granting of the one demand that more than any other had animated the civil rights movement: one man, one vote in local elections. It meant the end of the ratepayer vote and the company vote, each of which overwhelmingly favoured unionists. It granted universal adult suffrage in place of the old arrangements.

The same legislation began the process of dismantling gerrymandered boundaries. It also broadened the base of the electorate by extending the vote, at both and local and parliamentary elections, to eighteen-year-olds.

In all formal senses, Northern Ireland seemed to be entering the modern world in the autumn and early winter of 1969. However, too much had happened in that disastrous year for mere administrative reform to remedy. A year earlier, following Terence O'Neill's 'Crossroads' speech, there had been a burst of euphoria and optimism: the Dublin *Sunday Independent* nominated O'Neill as its man of the year. Now O'Neill and all he stood for had been swept under the receding wave. The reforms were in place, the worst injustices addressed, other reforms were in hand.

But even in the short run, it was not enough. Things were quickening – disastrously.

The IRA Split

On 28 December 1969, a body calling itself the Provisional Army Council issued a statement: 'In view of a decision by a majority of delegates at an unrepresentative convention of the IRA to recognise the British, Six-County and Twenty-Six-County parliaments, we, the minority of delegates at that convention … do hereby repudiate that compromising position and re-affirm the fundamental Republican position … The adoption of the compromising policy referred to is the logical outcome of an obsession in recent years with parliamentary politics with the consequent undermining of the basic military role of the Irish Republican Army. The failure to provide the maximum defence possible of our people in Belfast is ample evidence of this neglect.'

It was a coup. For many republicans, it was a renewal of baptismal vows, casting out all the modish socialism of the 1960s and refocusing on what really mattered. What mattered was the army: a fighting force that would drive the British out of Ireland for once and for all. In the meantime, it would defend 'our people'. There was no mistaking who 'our people' were, any more than there was any confusion when unionists spoke of the 'people of Ulster'. These were two distinct people, and they did not like each other.

The Provos were at least realistic. The Officials – as the socialist element now became – were not. Northern Ireland was a sectarian cockpit, and if July 1969 had proved anything, it was that faraway theory and secular aspiration were of no use in the face of murderous mobs.

Official IRA mobile patrol in Turf Lodge housing estate, Belfast. The patrol was a reaction to the death of local IRA leader, Joe McCann, the previous day in the Markets Area in a confrontation with soldiers and police.

Sinn Féin Ard Fheis

Barely a fortnight after the split in the IRA, a similar and parallel breach occurred in Sinn Féin – the political arm of the movement. At an ard fheis (convention) in Dublin, a vote was taken to end abstentionism and take seats in Dublin, Belfast and Westminster. This was the view of the party leadership, reflecting that of the military leadership, whose similar initiative had triggered the army split and given birth to the Provisional IRA.

That division now bled into the political wing. The vote to end abstention was carried, but by a majority insufficient to trigger the change of policy: it fell short of the two-thirds required. The large minority on the losing side promptly walked out and established Provisional Sinn Féin, taking offices on the other side of the city to the socialists, who now became Official Sinn Féin, just as the army faction which they controlled – or, more realistically, which controlled them – became the Official IRA.

In time, the Officials, politicians and military alike, were to lose this contest decisively. Apart from the greater realism of the Provisionals, given the desperate situation in Northern Ireland, their appeal was also to a more socially conservative sensibility among republicans, many of whom were unhappy with the nascent secularism and liberalism of the Republic in the 1960s. They regarded the Officials' policies as part of this social shift, an abandonment of old republican truths in favour of a trendy secularism of which they were deeply suspicious.

Arthur Griffith, third leader of Sinn Féin and later President of Dáil Éireann, who died in August 1922. The party was founded by Griffith in 1905. It subsequently became a focus for various forms of Irish nationalism, especially Irish republicanism. It suffered splits during the Irish Civil War in 1922, then again at the beginning of the Troubles in 1969. Today Sinn Féin is a republican, populist party.

Ballymurphy

There was a curious stand-off between the British Army and the nationalist population in the early weeks of 1970. The memory of the army as the deliverers of Catholics from Protestant mobs was still fresh.

This mural in Belfast commemorates the victims of the Ballymurphy Massacre in 1971, when 11 unarmed civilians were killed by British soldiers. The mural is by public artist R. Ó Murchú.

Most of the trouble that the army attracted came from the Protestant side, still smarting at reforms.

BALLYMURPHY MASSACRE
AUGUST 1971
WE DEMAND THE TRUTH

F. QUINN H. MULLAN

J. CONNOLLY D. TEGGART N. PHILIPS

J. MURPHY P. McCARTHY E. DOHERTY

J. LAVERTY J. CORR J. McKERR

But there were incidents in Derry in late March when a 1916 Rising commemoration sparked violence and arrests. Then, on 1 April, the UDR was formally established with an initial strength of 4,000 men.

On 31 March, a march of Junior Orangemen passed along the nationalist Springfield Road and was attacked. This developed into three nights of full-scale rioting centred on the Ballymurphy estate. The army arrived in force: 600 men and five Saracen armoured cars. The rioters threw missiles and bottles; the army fired 104 CS gas canisters. The army GOC, Sir Ian Freeland, announced a new 'get tough' policy, which entailed the army rampaging through the district, damaging property, shouting insults and arresting anyone they could. Naturally, loyalist gangs invaded under cover of the troops.

Meanwhile, in the nearby New Barnsley estate, Protestants were expelled from their homes by a nationalist mob, a reversal of the previous victim status. Suddenly, things looked rather more complex than a plea for civil rights from the righteously downtrodden.

The Ballymurphy riots acted as a recruiting sergeant for the Provisional IRA. Pleas from both Sir Arthur Young and General Freeland to ban all provocative parades were ignored at Stormont; to be fair, such a ban was probably not politically possible in the real world of Northern Ireland.

Ian Paisley MP

In mid-April 1970, there were two by-elections for Stormont, the more consequential one being in Bannside in County Antrim, the seat formerly held by Terence O'Neill, now Lord O'Neill of the Maine and removed to the House of Lords. He had been run close in Bannside in the Crossroads election by Ian Paisley, who now took the vacant seat with ease under the Protestant unionist banner.

Paisley was no ordinary politician. He was a mob orator of formidable power and gave the loudest possible voice to all that was fearful, bigoted and reactionary in the Ulster unionist tradition. The Unionist Party grandees affected to find him vulgar – which indeed he was – but he would eventually grow his support into the unionist mainstream.

At this point, however, Paisley was still on the margins. His long-standing opposition to any concessions were reflected in his campaign slogan, 'O'Neill Must Go' (because of the former prime minister's temporising). In November 1968, he successfully blocked a civil rights march in Armagh city centre by mobilising 30 cars and mustering supporters, some of whom carried guns and sundry other weapons including scythes, billhooks and, in one case, a sock filled with lead which poleaxed a television cameraman. This was the offence for which Paisley did his penitential and politically profitable three months in jail.

Two months later, another by-election delivered Paisley to Westminster for North Antrim and in the following year he set up the DUP, in direct opposition to the establishment Unionist Party.

Ian Paisley in 2007.
He died in 2014.

The Alliance Party

Also in April 1970, the Alliance Party was launched. It sought to identify the non-sectarian middle ground in Northern Ireland and to draw votes from both communities. It was the kind of centrist party that might have dominated, or at least been influential, in a normal polity. It attracted early support from pro-O'Neill unionists who acknowledged the need for reforms. Nationalist support was more hesitant but it was there. Alliance was a classically middle-class party: temperate, non-ideological, rational and, most of all, non-sectarian.

Sir Oliver Napier, leader of the Alliance Party 1972–84.

It made a decent showing in its first electoral outing – the district council elections of 1973 – when it achieved 13.6 per cent of the total vote. By then, it had acquired a Catholic as its leader. Oliver

Napier was a Belfast solicitor, an impressive and unflappable figure.

The Alliance Party is still there, a constant minority presence in the zero-sum world of Northern Ireland politics. There were times, over the years, when it nearly disappeared from the electoral map, but it endured because it represented something real, a desire among a minority for a regime of bourgeois virtue. Numerically, this was a lost cause – Alliance never polled 20 per cent in any subsequent election – but it gave public substance to a desire for accommodation and a voice to a stabilising social group that was disproportionately capable of delivering it. It was influential both in the later Sunningdale and Belfast Agreements. It did not live in vain.

A United Ulster Unionist poster, warning that the Sunningdale Agreement would lead to a united Ireland.

The Dublin Arms Trial

In Dublin, the northern crisis had thrown the government party, Fianna Fáil, into confusion. Rhetorically republican, in practice it was a coalition of moderates – who paid lip service to republican pieties but were actually more concerned with administration and office – and true believers, not all of whom were marginal figures in the party. The Troubles quickly opened a fissure between these two elements.

Jack Lynch, 1967.

In early 1970, Taoiseach Jack Lynch learned of a plot to import arms in support of the Provisional IRA and that members of the cabinet were involved. Lynch promptly sacked Neil Blaney – a hardline republican – and Charles Haughey, the minister for finance. Haughey was not thought to have any particular republican leanings – other than the usual pious rhetoric – but rather to be dedicated to the secular and political advancement of his own career. This perception was not wrong but there were clearly depths to Haughey as yet undiscovered. A third minister, Kevin Boland, from the backwoods republican wing, resigned in protest.

A criminal trial followed in which Blaney, Haughey, an army officer and a businessman were all acquitted. The trial judge declared that one of the two ministers must have perjured themselves, although he could not say which. The whole situation demonstrated the capacity of the Northern Ireland poison to infect the rest of the island. In the end, Jack Lynch's actions – although themselves ambiguous – brought victory for the moderates in Fianna Fáil and resulted in the marginalisation of the hawks. Haughey faced the best part of a decade in the wilderness.

Charles Haughey, June 1967.

The Macrory Report

GOVERNMENT OF NORTHERN IRELAND

REVIEW BODY
ON
LOCAL GOVERNMENT
IN NORTHERN IRELAND
1970

CHAIRMAN: PATRICK A. MACRORY, ESQ.

REPORT

*Presented to Parliament by Command of
His Excellency the Governor of Northern Ireland
June 1970*

BELFAST
HER MAJESTY'S STATIONERY OFFICE

The official report.

One of the key demands of the civil rights movement had been the reform of local government. At the end of May 1970, a report produced by a committee headed by Sir Patrick Macrory, a barrister, recommended the abolition of the existing system based on the six counties and its replacement by 26 district councils. Other services, such as health, education and the public library system, would be similarly devolved to local district boards.

Unsurprisingly, existing councillors opposed the reforms, being quite content with the old system. But the Stormont government accepted the recommendations anyway. The new structures came into being after the local elections of 1973 and were further refined later.

The system was intended to be run by the Northern Ireland parliament. But that body was not long for this world, and the post-Sunningdale assembly did not last long either. The net effect was that the new local district structures became part of the direct rule apparatus, thus creating a democratic deficit. Unionists in particular were much exercised by this deficit, discovering an affection for representative democracy not always vivid in their culture hitherto. In truth, local politicians were emasculated, reduced to responsibility for little more than refuse collection, public toilets and the burial or cremation of the dead, powers characterised as 'bins, bogs and burials'. A process that was supposed to have enabled local agency in fact emptied it of content, a nice example of the law of unintended consequences.

'Belfast Says No' banner in front of City Hall, Belfast.

Ted Heath in Downing Street

Against most predictions, the Tories under Ted Heath won the British general election of 1970, the election that delivered Paisley to Westminster. In the opposite direction, it brought Reginald Maudling, who now replaced Callaghan as home secretary, to Northern Ireland.

For his first visit, he was in and out in a day. He didn't like it: 'For God's sake, bring me a large scotch; what a bloody awful country.' Like Callaghan, he quickly reckoned that there was no cure for what ailed the province. That, combined, with the Tories' perennial inclination towards law-and-order solutions, would have malign consequences.

Maudling's famous remark, born of the frustration of having his ears bashed by importuning supplicants on all sides, was perhaps the most eloquent marker

Tory leader Edward Heath after the count at his constituency of Bexley Heath, June 1970.

of a difference that unionists knew in their hearts to be true and Tories denied to themselves: Northern Ireland was another country. There was hypocrisy all round. Unionists insisted with equal force that Northern Ireland was as British as Sussex, while trying to preserve as many of their exceptional usages as London would now allow them. London talked about the sanctity of the union, while regarding Ulster as a foreign madhouse. Dublin said it wanted unity and would have been horrified to have it offered to them.

The situation, already bad, began to spin out of control. The Provisional IRA resolved on a war of choice and began their long, fruitless insurgency. The Tories upped the law-and-order stakes. They were chicken and egg to each other.

Home Secretary Reginald Maudling gets a first hand view of Ulster's problems, as he talks to troops off the Falls Road in 1970.

Bernadette Devlin in Jail

Bernadette Devlin had become a world-famous figure in the Derry riots that followed the Burntollet march and those triggered by the Apprentice Boys' march in August which became the Battle of the Bogside. She was young, telegenic and torrentially eloquent: she might have been made for an era sympathetic to left-leaning revolutionary causes and where television – the wonder of the age – brought even the most remote places into quiet suburban living rooms.

The idea that the nationalist insurgency in Northern Ireland was part of a universal pattern – the civil rights movement in America, civil unrest in Paris, the Prague Spring and all the other similar events – was one that has never quite gone away. In later years, Sinn Féin, in particular, proved themselves extremely clever in using buzzwords that appealed to this sensibility. But before it was anything else, the trouble in Northern Ireland was not new; it was the revival of an old, ethno-religious quarrel that would have embarrassed the radical chic. Most northern nationalists were socially conservative.

Devlin had been sentenced to six months for her 1969 activities and had appealed. The appeal was rejected and in June 1970 she was arrested at a road block and taken to Armagh Women's Prison to begin her sentence (she served four months). Her imprisonment was the prompt for more rioting in Derry, although from now the action moved to Belfast. It was a downward spiral rather than a revolutionary dawn.

Bernadette Devlin leaving the court in Derry.

The Short Strand

The day after Bernadette Devlin went to jail, 27 June 1970, there was sustained and vicious rioting in North and East Belfast. That part of the city east of the River Lagan is overwhelmingly Protestant but the Short Strand – close to the river and the city centre – is a tiny Catholic enclave, an island in a Protestant sea. Its parish church is St Malachy's, whose spire dominates the local area. Surrounded by the tribal enemy, the Short Strand is especially vulnerable to attack and by now loyalists had acquired an appetite for sectarian assault.

They came on 27 June. But the nascent Provisional IRA (PIRA) had found a few men who, armed with guns, used St Malachy's to defend the area. By the time it was over, five Protestants were dead, along with one Catholic. The action lasted for five hours. It was the first serious outing by a PIRA unit and it stood in stark and exemplary contrast to the invertebrate response in West Belfast the previous summer. Communal defence was henceforth the imperative. There would be no more 'IRA: I Ran Away'.

The IRA embarked on a self-declared war to run the British out of Ireland. But who were the British? It wasn't the British army, which did not want to be there. It was the Ulster Protestants, who did. The

Provisionals were never able to disentangle the sectarian necessity from the national aspiration. It was no accident that this first flexing of their muscles was in a defensive cause and that their victims were their fellow Irishmen, albeit of the 'wrong sort'.

Protestant youths in Belfast play under windows shattered by IRA sniper fire in 1970.

The Falls Curfew

The summer and autumn of 1970 saw the situation deteriorate even further. As late as September, loyalist mobs on the Shankill Road placed a British army post under siege for a full three days: if the army could not pacify loyalists, what hope had they against republicans? The fraternisation of the previous year – grounded in the sheer relief in Catholic areas that the British army was there at all – was long gone. Now the army was increasingly regarded as an army of occupation, as atavistic Anglophobia reasserted itself in nationalist minds.

Far from being the quick in-and-out operation originally promised by Jim Callaghan, the army's presence was by now a part of the political furniture. Little as they cared for the loyalists – one army commander sneered at 'grown men' marching around in Orange regalia – it was inevitably nationalists who came to be regarded as the primary enemy. The loyalists, for all their absurdities, were still waving the flag under which the army fought. The nationalists, and the republicans in particular, wanted shot of that flag.

The final alienation came in July 1970. After serious rioting and civil disturbance, the army imposed a 34-hour curfew on the Lower Falls area of West Belfast, solidly republican in allegiance. The curfew covered about 50 streets and was patrolled by an overhead helicopter. Searches of houses turned up weapons, firearms, bombs and bomb-making equipment, ammunition and two-way radios. Residents complained of army brutality. There were gunfights that killed five people and injured 60. The curfew also killed any residual idea that the British army was the protector of Catholic communities.

Opposite: Mural on Divis Street in remembrance of the Falls Curfew, Belfast, Northern Ireland, May 2011.

The SDLP

The Crossroads election of 1969 more or less finished off the old Nationalist Party. Its leader, Eddie McAteer, was beaten in the Foyle constituency of Derry by John Hume, who had come to prominence in the early civil rights movement. Just as the pressure of events impelled the republicans to split and re-group, now the constitutional nationalists faced a similar necessity.

The Social Democratic and Labour Party (SDLP) was formed in August 1970 out of the remains of the Nationalist Party, together with various labour and independent nationalists. Its primary aim was the peaceful reunification of Ireland, pending which its emphasis was on increasing equality within Northern Ireland.

Its first leader was Gerry Fitt, the tough, funny ex-docker who had done so much to educate the British Labour Party about Ulster realities and who had received honourable battle wounds in Derry in October 1968. His deputy was Hume, who was the political brains of the party. Where Fitt was a charming maverick, Hume was a patient, almost pedagogic, organisation man. They might have made a complementary pair; instead there were tensions from the off. The conservative nationalists, especially outside Belfast, were never

comfortable with the socialist rhetoric, albeit it was
relatively muted.

Nonetheless, the SDLP gave constitutional
nationalism a structure and a sense of purpose.
For a generation, it represented a clear majority of
nationalist opinion until eventually displaced by
Sinn Féin, rather as the DUP would displace the
Ulster Unionists.

Stormont MP John
Hume seen here at the
inauguration of Northern
Ireland's alternative
parliament at Dungiven,
November 1971.

Civil Violence, 1970

Neither the Stormont government under Chichester-Clark, nor the Tories in London under Heath and Maudling (soon to be outed as a crook) nor the British army on the ground were able to contain the growing violence. While headline moments such as the Falls Curfew are most prominent, it was the relentless drip of minor incidents that marked the growing descent into the abyss.

Maudling tried to get the Orange Order to call off its traditional July parades. They declined, and on 13 July a bomb in a bank in central Belfast injured 30 people. The Stormont government then introduced a parades ban for six months. The army shot dead a young man, precipitating more riots. Rubber bullets were deployed for the first time. In August two RUC men died in a booby-trap bomb in Crossmaglen, a republican stronghold in South Armagh hard on the border.

An IRA man blew himself up when trying to place a bomb in a Belfast electricity transformer. In late October, there were three nights of rioting in the Catholic Ardoyne area of West Belfast. Sir Arthur Young resigned as chief constable of the RUC, no doubt glad to get away from the mayhem and back

British Army issue 37mm-calibre rubber bullets, as used during the Troubles in Northern Ireland.

to England. The fragile civil society of Northern Ireland was fracturing and no one had any idea what to do to stop this. Yet it never entirely collapsed: one of the things least remarked about the coming years, with all their miseries and needless deaths, was that some version of civil society held together. Northern Ireland was bad, but it was never Lebanon. There was still some sort of solid centre.

Jumbled sign after a bomb blast in Belfast, May 1972.

Prime Minister Faulkner

The dismal toll of violence and murder continued into the early months of 1971. There was rioting in republican areas of West Belfast but also on the loyalist Shankill Road. On 6 February, the PIRA shot the first British soldier to die in the conflict. Two days later, an army vehicle knocked down and killed a five-year-old girl, sparking further rioting.

The next day, five men, including two BBC engineers, were killed by a landmine in County Tyrone. Two RUC men died in an IRA attack in Belfast. That was just the toll for February. In the middle of all that, the Housing Executive Act (Northern Ireland) 1971 came into force, addressing a key civil rights demand. Hardly anyone noticed.

What everyone noticed was the chaos on the streets. Few noticed it more loudly than Ian Paisley, now accusing the Stormont government of 'pussy-footing and fence-straddling' and calling daily for Chichester-Clark's resignation. In March, he got his wish. Chichester-Clark flew to London to see Heath, who offered him every assistance short of help. Chichester-Clark resigned and was replaced by Brian Faulkner, a bourgeois who had long failed to conceal his ambition.

In the meantime, there were gun battles between the Official and Provisional IRA, as each faction sought dominance. The Provisionals won in the long term but in the short term too: each side held their own commemorations of the 1916 Easter Rising.

1972 saw an explosion of political violence in Northern Ireland, when nearly 500 people lost their lives. Unionists claim the main reason was the formation of the Provisional Irish Republican Army (PIRA).

Internment

The violence continued. One long-remembered incident in March was the killing of three off-duty soldiers, two of them brothers, lured from a pub by young women, handed over to the PIRA and executed in cold blood. Faulkner started his premiership by announcing a few reforms, liberal by Northern Ireland standards, albeit unremarkable anywhere else.

Meanwhile the violence continued, seemingly out of control, and the summer marching season approached. Republican provocations increased, while on the loyalist sides 'tartan gangs' began to form in reprisal. By early May there had been 136 gelignite explosions in the province since the beginning of the year. In July, there were severe riots in Derry, in which two men were shot dead. John Hume demanded an enquiry and, when none was forthcoming, the SDLP withdrew from Stormont.

HMS *Maidstone*, a 1930s warship, was moored at Belfast and used as a prison ship.

Faulkner was in an impossible position but he now made a catastrophic miscalculation, albeit with Heath's permission. On 9 August 1971, the government introduced internment without trial. The security information on which it was based was out of date and most senior republicans escaped the net. Innocents who were interned were radicalised. It was the best recruiting sergeant that the IRA could have dreamed of: violence spiked. Prior to internment, 34 people had died in Troubles-related incidents; after internment, the figure was 140. In the Ballymurphy area of Belfast alone, 11 civilians, including a priest, were shot dead between 9–11August.

In all, 174 people died in violence in 1971, compared to 25 in 1970. It was about to get worse.

The entrance to Compound 19 of the Long Kesh Internment Camp in 2006, six years after it had closed.

Bloody Sunday

On 30 January 1972, a civil rights march in Derry drew an attendance of more than 10,000 people. The government had banned the march but it was ignored. The march was to protest against internment. Also present, in support of the police, was the 1st battalion of the Parachute Regiment. What this ferocious unit was doing anywhere near a police operation – even one in an environment where for months the IRA had been attacking army units – was anyone's guess. The RUC wanted them held back. The army, gung-ho for revenge, sent them in. The result was the murder of 13 men and one woman, all innocents.

Bloody Sunday was shocking in its scale, its ruthlessness and its recklessness, and it was done in cold blood by the army of the alleged sovereign power. The army claimed that it had been fired on first. A whitewash by a British judge endorsed this view and it took more than 30 years and an immense amount of money for another judge to uncover the truth. The paras had been sent in to teach the Paddies a lesson.

The alienation of northern Catholics was complete. World opinion turned against the British in disgust. The British embassy in Dublin was burned by a mob. Bernadette Devlin MP, who had been in Derry that day, marched across the floor of the House of Commons, pulled Maudling's hair, slapped his face and called him a liar for saying the troops had been fired at. 'I did not shoot him in the back, which is what they did to our people.'

Troops rounding up
people at the march.

Direct Rule

Nothing could possibly be the same again after the seismic shock of Bloody Sunday. Some old patterns continued: William Craig, the former Stormont minister, set up a loyalist ginger group called Vanguard and drew 70,000 to a rally in East Belfast. Paisley called for the establishment of a third force, a neo-fascist militia. The IRA continued bombing, including one particular and long-remembered explosion in Belfast's Abercorn restaurant which killed two people and injured 130. Two of the injured were sisters, shopping for a wedding dress. Both were horribly mutilated; one losing both legs, and the bride-to-be both legs, her right arm and one of her eyes.

But this was now a kind of dismal business as usual. After Bloody Sunday, even Heath and Maudling had to concede that time was up for devolved government in Northern Ireland. It demanded that control of law and order be returned to London. Stormont refused – its very reason for existence had always lain in control of local security – and London first prorogued it and then shut it down completely. It met for the last time on 28 March 1972.

A new British cabinet position, secretary of state for Northern Ireland, was established. Its first occupant, assisted by junior ministers, was William Whitelaw, who was later to prosper as Margaret Thatcher's right-hand man. The Northern Ireland civil service was likewise integrated with Whitehall.

The IRA regarded direct rule as a victory. On no evidence at all, they saw it as a staging post to a united Ireland by isolating British rule in its 'true' colonial context. As usual, this analysis ignored the Brits on the ground, the local Protestants. Direct rule may have been the end of the Orange state; it was not the end of the Troubles.

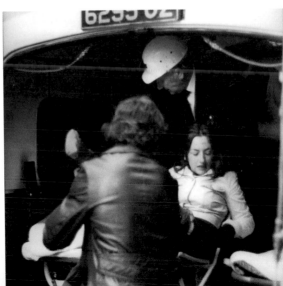

A young victim being helped into an ambulance after the Abercorn restaurant explosion. Glass showered over pavements packed with people. About 20 of the injured, most of them women and children, were very seriously hurt.

Bloody Friday

The violence continued. The Official IRA murdered a Derry man home on leave from the British army, thus outraging local opinion and further relegating it relative to the Provos. On 29 May, it announced a ceasefire. The Provos did not. Back-channel manoeuvres resulted in a secret meeting in London between Whitelaw and representatives of the IRA, including Gerry Adams, released from jail specially to be in attendance. It was a dialogue of the deaf.

On 21 July, the IRA committed its most concerted series of murderous attacks to date. In Belfast, it set off 26 bombs which killed 11 innocent people and injured more than 130 others. Some of the dead were so mutilated that their body parts were scraped up into plastic bags. There was other violence that day, bombs and gun battles, but it was the coordinated nature of the murders that horrified nationalist Ireland and filled it with shame. After the moral simplicities of Bloody Sunday, the tangled moral nuance of Bloody Friday: this was the moment when the IRA and republicanism condemned itself to the margins. They were no longer respectable. Many nationalists who had given them the benefit of the doubt now withdrew it. There was a fascist streak in republicanism, now in plain sight.

At 2:48 pm, a car bomb exploded outside the Ulsterbus depot in Oxford Street, the busiest bus station in Northern Ireland.

Later that evening, a Catholic innocent was kidnapped by loyalists and horribly done to death by a gang subsequently dubbed the Shankill Butchers. Even by the standards of the depravity into which the province was now sinking, the Shankill Butchers were to prove themselves psychopathic.

Sunningdale

The campaign went on. The British army ended no-go areas in Belfast and Derry, for what it was worth. There was rioting at every excuse and none. There were talks and conferences. Special non-jury courts were established to obviate the intimidation of prosecution witnesses. But 1972 proved the nadir of the Troubles, at least as far as deaths were concerned: 470 people lost their lives in that terrible year.

On 1 January 1973, the UK and Ireland both joined the EEC. Then two Protestants were interned on suspicion of murder. This outraged loyalists, who responded by calling a general strike, enforced by armed bullies. The lights went out in Belfast. A policeman and a fireman were killed. The organisers congratulated the 'grassroots', but respectable unionist opinion was horrified at seeing such power in the hands of thugs.

The government produced a white paper recommending a new assembly at Stormont, elected by PR and with a power-sharing devolved government. This made many unionists uneasy, to say the least, but Faulkner got approval from the Ulster Unionist Council. Elections were duly held, returning Faulkner's unionists as the largest group. Overall, the pro-white-paper candidates won a majority.

Eventually, an executive was formed.

A conference then took place in Sunningdale, near London, with representatives of the Belfast power-sharing executive and the London and Dublin governments present. It aimed to create an institutional framework within which power-sharing could work. This involved cross-border cooperation: there was to be a council of Ireland to discuss matters of mutual concern. Dublin pushed harder for this than was wise, for Faulkner could not sell it to his base, as events soon demonstrated.

Stormont.

The Northern Ireland Executive

Sunningdale was the high point of optimism in the early days of the Troubles. It seemed as if a broad consensus had been found where moderates from every side could find common ground. Its headline achievements were impressive: people who might barely have acknowledged each other's presence five years earlier had cobbled together some sort of a deal. And, for a short while, it worked. New institutions were born. The Northern Ireland Executive took shape.

The executive comprised 11 senior ministers: six from the Ulster Unionist Party (UUP), four SDLP and one Alliance. Faulkner was chief executive and Fitt was his deputy. In structural terms, it was a rational solution to a divided society, but Northern Ireland, in common with most divided societies, was high on emotion and low on rationalism. Republicans regarded the SDLP as quislings and even before they left Sunningdale, Faulkner and his colleagues were concerned about the likely loyalist reaction to having a party like the SDLP, whose primary declared objective was still reunification, in government at all.

Alas, the devil is as much in the timing as in the detail. It was all very sensible, but too much too soon. For many Protestants, everything that had happened in the previous five years had represented either a retreat or an outright defeat. Now this: a council of Ireland which was a stalking horse for reunification. Loyalists mobilised, forming the Ulster Army Council as an umbrella group for its various paramilitaries. The PIRA set off bombs in London. The executive was hamstrung for the duration of its short life. All it did was give a glimpse of possibility for the future. There could have been no greater symbolic indication that the Orange state was dead than to see nationalists in government.

Stormont Castle.

The 1974 Election & the UWC Strike

Heath's Tory government had turned into a shambles and he called a general election in February 1974. As usual, Northern Ireland was the last thing on their minds. An election that in Britain turned on the three-day week, the miners' strike and the chant of 'who governs Britain?', in Northern Ireland became a referendum on the nascent executive, barely two months old.

The key result was within unionism. The pro-assembly unionists under Faulkner polled a miserable 13.1 per cent of the vote. Alliance could only scratch 3.2 per cent. On the other hand, the United Ulster Unionist Council (UUUC), which had been set up the previous month to mobilise all anti-Sunningdale unionists on the grounds that the agreement was a first step to reunification, took 51.1 per cent of the votes and 11 of the 12 Westminster seats (the 12th going to Gerry Fitt). Faulkner remained chief executive for the moment but had been kicked out as UUP leader, to be replaced by Harry West. Faulkner was now a political orphan.

In May, a body calling itself the Ulster Workers' Council (UWC) organised a general strike. It cut off power supplies and strangled economic activity across the province. It was supported by thugs who set up road blocks and intimidated people. In Dublin, three bombs killed 22 people; loyalist paramilitaries denied responsibility but no one believed them. Facing intolerable pressure, unionist members of the executive resigned, collapsing it. There would not be a similar representative institution in Northern Ireland for a generation.

In May 1974 the militant Protestants of the Ulster Worker's Council, organisers of the general strike in the province, refused to provide even skeleton essential services. They intensified the stoppage after troops took over oil and petrol storage depots and 21 filling stations.

Birmingham & Guildford

Faulkner resigned on 28 May. The death of the executive was the death of politics in Northern Ireland, at least until further notice. That left only the paramilitaries. To the amazement of the Provos, direct rule had not proved a stepping stone to reunification. On the contrary, the British appeared to be going nowhere. The PIRA thus took the war to the mainland, to remind them of the price to be paid for such incomprehensible intransigence.

The destruction after the bomb in Birmingham.

All through 1974, there were various PIRA bombings in England, including one that destroyed a coach on the M62, killing nine soldiers. Then, on 5 October, two no-warning bombs exploded in pubs in Guildford, killing five people – including two soldiers – and injuring 54. Far worse followed in Birmingham in November. Again, it was two bombs in pubs. This time, the dead numbered 21 and there were almost 200 people injured, some of them very severely.

What followed was tragedy rather than farce. Ten Irish men were convicted of the two bombings and all served long sentences. All were innocent, as was eventually proved. It was probably the lowest moment in the history of English criminal law. In the case of the Birmingham Six, their innocence was established principally by a heroic English journalist and later Labour MP and distinguished political diarist, Chris Mullin. The IRA knew who the real bombers were but their honour code precluded them from any collaboration with the authorities, so they let the innocents rot.

Paddy Hill in 2015. The Birmingham Six were six Irishmen: Hugh Callaghan, Patrick Joseph Hill, Gerard Hunter, Richard McIlkenny, William Power and John Walker, who, in 1975, were each sentenced to life imprisonment following their false convictions for the Birmingham pub bombings.

The IRA Truce

In December 1974, an extraordinary meeting took place in faraway Feakle, County Clare, between six members of the PIRA army council and some Protestant clergymen. As a result, the IRA declared a temporary ceasefire, which in turn led to a truce. Early in the new year, secret talks between PIRA and officials of the Northern Ireland Office (NIO) appeared to have led to a draft agreement. The NIO denied this, although a document found on a captured IRA leader, Dáithí Ó Conaill, in Dublin suggested otherwise.

Dáithí Ó Conaill, vice-president of Republican Sinn Féin. It is thought he introduced the car bomb to Northern Ireland.

The truce held, with twitchy moments, for most of 1975. It is not clear that the British ever seriously considered a withdrawal from Northern Ireland, although Secretary of State Merlyn Rees later confirmed that the possibility had been discussed at cabinet. It would be surprising had it not been. The Provos were, as ever, fixated on the idea that direct rule was a stepping stone to a united Ireland. It was a feeling shared in an equal and opposite way by many loyalists dreaming of a return to the Orange state. The UUUC was quite open about this ambition.

The truce did not mean the end of all violence. Only one soldier died but other killings, mainly sectarian, continued. There was also feuding between paramilitary groups on both sides which accounted for fatalities. Indeed, more people died in the first nine months of 1975 than in the equivalent period in 1974. In all, 247 died in the year of the truce, an increase of 27 on the preceding year.

Welsh-born Merlyn Rees, Labour MP from 1963 until 1992, served as secretary of state for Northern Ireland (1974–76) and home secretary (1976–79).

War on the Mainland

The truce, such as it was, mainly applied to the IRA and the British army in Northern Ireland. For the most part, it worked until it finally fell away in the autumn of 1975. However, this did not inhibit the PIRA from continuing their campaign in Britain itself. In January four bombs exploded in London, while another in Manchester injured 19. In February, an IRA man shot a London policeman in cold blood; in the police follow-up, they uncovered an IRA bomb factory in Hammersmith.

In October, one person died and many were injured in a bomb explosion at Green Park underground station. Then a car bomb exploded outside the home of Hugh Fraser, a Tory MP, which killed a passer-by, leaving Fraser unscathed. In November, two died and 23 were injured in an explosion in a London restaurant. Ross McWhirter, a supporter of right-wing causes and co-founder of the *Guinness Book of Records*, was murdered by republican gunmen. Finally, and most dramatic of all, the police raided an IRA cell in a flat in Balcombe Street, just off the Marylebone Road in central London. Four IRA men took a married couple hostage while the police besieged the flat for six days. The IRA men's demands for safe passage back to Ireland was refused and eventually they were starved out.

It is hard to discern what the IRA thought all this might achieve in a city that had survived the Luftwaffe. Increasingly, it became clear that rational strategy was not always the first item on the agenda of a cult, and militant republicanism is just that: a cult.

10 December 1975: police use a semaphore language by using two flags, one red and the other green for officers entering or leaving the siege building in Balcombe Street, Marylebone, in which IRA gunmen are holding a middle-aged man and his wife hostage in their flat.

Kingsmills

The beginning of 1976 was gruesome even by the standards of Northern Ireland. On 4 January, two Catholics were murdered at their home near Whitecross, County Armagh. Three Catholics were killed by Protestant gunmen across the county border in Ballydugan, County Down.

The following morning, a bus carrying 11 workers was stopped at a road block at Kingsmills, not far from Whitecross. The workers were all Protestant, the driver Catholic. The Protestants, believing at first that this was a loyalist road block, tried to protect the driver. He was separated from the others and told to walk away and not look back. He fully expected a bullet in the back. But these were local republicans, styling themselves the Republican Action Force – a code name for the local IRA.

The bullet-riddled bus following the Kingsmills attack.

As he walked away, the driver heard the repeated sound of machine-gun fire. Ten of the Protestant workers were murdered where they stood. One man – severely wounded – survived to tell the tale.

County Armagh, the orchard county, is beautiful. But it has had a singular history. Nowhere else in Ulster has been such a concentrated sectarian cockpit, with numbers of Catholics, Anglicans and Presbyterians so closely matched in such proximity. It was the county where the Orange Order was founded in 1795. It lived by its own rules. There was a terrible reckoning behind this appalling atrocity: there were no more sectarian murders in County Armagh that year.

Portrait of William III (1650–702), Prince of Orange, by Peter Lely. The Loyal Orange Institution, known as the Orange Order, is a Protestant fraternal order in Northern Ireland. Its name is a tribute to the Dutch-born Protestant King William of Orange, who defeated the army of Catholic King James II in the Williamite-Jacobite War of 1688-91. It was founded in County Armagh in 1795, during a period of Protestant-Catholic sectarian conflict, as a Masonic-style fraternity.

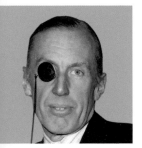

Christopher Ewart-Biggs, Britain's ambassador to Dublin, was killed when a landmine exploded under the embassy car as he was being driven by his chauffeur from the official residence. Fellow passenger and civil servant Judith Cooke, aged 26, was also killed. The driver and another civil servant were injured. At the battle of El Alamein in 1942 he lost his right eye and as a result he wore a smoked-glass monocle over an artificial eye.

The UUAC Strike

There was a marked increase in Troubles-related deaths in 1976 compared to 1975: 297 as against 247. The British ambassador to Dublin, Christopher Ewart-Biggs, was assassinated by a landmine. Gerry Fitt's home in Belfast was attacked by republican thugs. A runaway car in west Belfast killed two children and gave rise to a spontaneous movement, the Peace People. Special-category status was withdrawn from republican prisoners in the Maze prison, prompting the so-called 'blanket' or 'dirty protest', which eventually escalated to hunger strikes.

In May 1977, the United Unionist Action Group (UUAC), an umbrella group for loyalist vigilantes, tried a rerun of the UWC strike of 1974 that had collapsed the short-lived executive. With Ian Paisley to the fore, it wanted tougher law and order measures and a return to majority rule. Paisley promised to leave politics if the strike failed, a promise he failed to keep.

The strike failed. There was insufficient support from Protestant trade unionists, especially the power workers at the vital Ballylumford power station, which supplied two-thirds of the province's electricity. Protestants might have supported the declared aims of the strike but, unlike in 1974, they did not see an existential threat to the union. The new secretary of state, Roy Mason, a tough, no-nonsense Yorkshireman, managed the political response and ensured that the police stood up to intimidation. In general, there was not the same stomach for the fight in the unionist community at large. Unionist solidarity could, as in 1974, veto political proposals it regarded as fundamentally hostile to their interests, but it could not dictate positive government policy.

Officers examine the scene of devastation.

The Shankill Butchers

If there was a fascist streak in militant republicanism, language can hardly muster the resources to describe the depravity of loyalism at its worst. Deranged and psychopathic hardly do justice to the Shankill Butchers. They were a gang of mainly UVF men who terrorised North and West Belfast for most of the 1970s. Their modus operandi was to grab a random and wholly innocent Catholic victim – for no reason other than his Catholicism – and subject him to barbaric tortures before dispatching him by cutting his throat.

This was sectarian terrorism at its rawest. At least the IRA could argue that their crimes were in a political cause. With the Butchers, there was no such mitigation. It was hatred, pure and simple. The leader of this murder cult was one Lenny Murphy who, despite his Catholic-sounding surname, was from a staunchly Protestant and loyalist background. He was a career criminal from a young age and had served time. It was only after his release from prison in 1975 that the worst of the Butchers' crimes were perpetrated.

One of the gang had worked in a meat-processing plant from which he had stolen the tools of their gruesome trade. In all, they were reckoned to be responsible for the deaths of at least 30 people, some of them Protestants with whom the gang had some grievance or other, but mostly Catholics. Murphy was convicted of firearms offences and jailed but was not convicted of the murders he orchestrated. His accomplices were, however, and were handed down a total of 42 life sentences, making it the biggest murder trial in British legal history. When Murphy was released, he was promptly shot dead by the IRA.

A UVF mural on the Shankill Road, where the gang was based.

The Mountbatten Murders

The IRA had always dreamt of assassinating a senior member of the British royal family. On 27 August 1979, they got their wish. Lord Louis Mountbatten was a Royal Navy officer – an uncle of the Duke of Edinburgh and a cousin of the queen. He was especially close to Charles, Prince of Wales. He was the last British viceroy of India.

He had a holiday home in County Sligo and it was his practice to spend some time there every summer. He did not bother with a bodyguard or take any special security precautions, despite the proximity of the border with Northern Ireland. On the fateful day, he set out from the local harbour at Mullaghmore with his eldest daughter, her husband and mother-in-law, his two grandsons and a boat boy from County Fermanagh. The previous evening an IRA man had managed to attach a remote-controlled explosive to the bottom of the boat.

A short distance from the shore, the bomb was detonated. Mountbatten, one of his grandsons, his son-in-law's mother and the boat boy died. Two men were charged with the murders; one was acquitted, the other, Thomas McMahon, was convicted and sentenced to life imprisonment but was released in 1998 under the terms of the Good Friday agreement. On the same day that Mountbatten died, an ambush near Warrenpoint, County Down, killed 18 British army soldiers, the biggest loss sustained in a single day by the army during the Troubles.

Lord Mountbatten.

Warrenpoint, County Down.

A police officer examining the boat wreckage.

The Hunger Strikes

Paramilitary prisoners – and the IRA in particular – did not regard themselves as criminals. They therefore demanded special category status in prison, a concession that they had won from William Whitelaw in 1972. It meant that they could wear their own clothes, were excused from prison work and were permitted extra visits and food parcels. In effect, they became a self-governing colony within the prison. By the time the authorities tried to phase out special status in the late 1970s, the number of prisoners that were eligible for it had reached more than 1,500.

Republican prisoners continued to insist on special status. At first, they went 'on the blanket', refusing prison clothes and wrapping themselves in blankets. This escalated into the 'dirty protest', in which they smeared their cells with their

Commemorative mural.

own excreta. Finally, unable to move the British government, they went on hunger strike.

There were two hunger strikes, the first of which reached a negotiated settlement in December 1980. Inevitably, the settlement terms were ambiguous and many republicans cried betrayal. On 1 March 1981, a second strike began, led by Bobby Sands, serving 14 years for firearms offences. After 66 days on strike, Sands died on 5 May, having in the meantime been elected MP for Fermanagh-South Tyrone in a by-election. Nine more followed him before the strikes were finally called off in October. Special status continued in diluted form for another decade but the hunger strikes had a transformative effect. Sinn Féin began its long march towards politics. Slowly but steadily, it ate into the SDLP's nationalist vote.

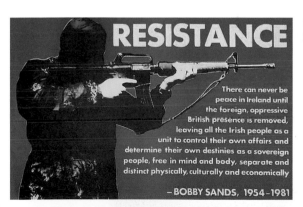

Poster quoting Bobby Sands.

Rolling Devolution

Following the melodrama of the hunger strikes, there was a feeling that some urgency needed to be injected into the politics of Northern Ireland. This idea was promoted by a new secretary of state, James Prior, a senior member of Margaret Thatcher's Tory government. The basic idea was called rolling devolution.

It envisaged an assembly elected by PR that would at first have limited powers, but which would acquire more as time went by and the new institutions bedded in. The assembly would require a weighted majority for major decisions, to ensure a degree of cross-community support.

James Prior at his desk.

Predictably, the unionist parties objected to this. They were still harking back to simple majoritarian – that is, Protestant – rule: the Orange state. The Alliance party welcomed the proposals as returning a degree of political autonomy to the province, but the SDLP opposed it because it made no allowance for an Irish dimension. For them, increasingly feeling the heat from Sinn Féin, any hint of an internal Northern Ireland settlement was unacceptable.

An assembly was duly elected and lasted in attenuated form for about four years. The non-cooperation of the nationalist parties rendered its cross-community aspirations void. It stumbled along, doing little of note other than providing public relations opportunities for politicians, until it was effectively superseded by a much more substantial arrangement. But at least rolling devolution had offered a glimpse of representative local politics after the dead years of direct rule. What came next, the Anglo-Irish Agreement, surprised many and enraged as many again. But first, the IRA very nearly succeeded in killing the entire British cabinet.

The Brighton Bomb

Margaret Thatcher.

In October 1984 the Conservative Party was holding its annual party conference in the Grand Hotel, Brighton. Margaret Thatcher, the party leader and prime minister since 1979, was approaching the height of her powers. She had the triumph of the Falklands behind her and the rout of the trade unions still to come.

Alan Clark, 1993.

At 2:54 in the morning, a 9-kg/20-lb IRA bomb destroyed the middle of the hotel, killing five people and injuring many others, some of them horribly. The prime minister herself narrowly escaped injury; two minutes earlier, she had been in a bathroom that was completely devastated by the bomb. Survivors stumbled, blinking and bemused, into the night. Alan Clark MP, in his diary, exclaimed: ' … what a coup for the Paddies … If they just had the wit to press their advantage, a couple of chaps with guns in the crowd, they could have got the whole government.'

As it was, the effect was electric. One MP died, as did the wife of a cabinet minister. One of the severely wounded was the wife of Norman Tebbit, a right-winger close to Thatcher. The IRA were unrepentant: 'Today, we were unlucky, but remember we only have to be lucky once. You have to be lucky always.'

Later that day, Thatcher appeared – not a hair out of place – and delivered her conference speech as if nothing had happened. There was no shortage of people who detested her abrasive personality, but very few who did not her admire her sheer sangfroid on that occasion.

Norman Tebbit in 2018. In 1984, he was injured in the bombing of the Grand Hotel. His wife Margaret was left permanently disabled after the explosion.

The Grand Hotel, Brighton, showing bomb damage.

The Anglo-Irish Agreement

While having little to do with Prior's rolling devolution, the SDLP instead participated in a body entitled the New Ireland Forum, under the aegis of the Dublin government of Garret FitzGerald. FitzGerald was anxious to bolster the SDLP against growing Sinn Féin support. The forum was a pan-nationalist discussion group, representing parties north and south but not Sinn Féin. It reiterated the traditional nationalist aspiration to a unitary state, but left open the possibility of a federal arrangement or joint authority. Thatcher immediately rejected all three options in the bluntest possible terms.

Poster used by the 1985 Ulster Says No protest campaign against the Anglo-Irish Agreement.

She did, however, agree to a series of meetings with FitzGerald, who impressed upon her the fact that unless northern nationalists felt that they held some stake in the country, all attempts at a purely security solution to the Troubles would founder. Both prime ministers deserve credit for what followed, Thatcher for putting the Brighton bomb behind her and FitzGerald for not being deflected by her sheer bad manners.

The outcome was a deal, the Anglo-Irish Agreement of 1985. While maintaining the existing constitutional position, it gave representatives of the Dublin government a consultative role in Northern Ireland affairs for the first time, thus recognising reality. Thatcher had lost patience with unionist intransigence and effectively did the deal over their heads. Naturally, they were incandescent, but they had over-played their hand. Had they allowed a degree of power-sharing under the rolling devolution regime, there would almost certainly have been no agreement. But in wanting it all, they were left with nothing. For the first time, nationalists felt that they had some voice in public affairs.

Garret FitzGerald and Margaret Thatcher at the signing of the Anglo-Irish Agreement in 1985.

Adams & McGuinness

Sinn Féin was the political wing of the IRA. At the party's 1982 ard fheis it was resolved that all party candidates must offer 'unambivalent support to the armed struggle'. However, by the mid-1980s, and after the trauma of the hunger strikes, it was clear that neither military victory nor defeat was in sight. This sense of a campaign going nowhere prompted a generational change at the top of Sinn Féin, as well as a shift from a southern to a northern leadership.

Sinn Féin president Gerry Adams, speaking to vice-president Martin McGuinness, at a party ard fheis.

Gerry Adams was the coming man in Sinn Féin. He had won the West Belfast Westminster seat from Gerry Fitt in 1983 and was elected party president later that year, defeating the outgoing leader, Ruairí Ó Brádaigh, a southerner. Three years later he prompted a split with the old leadership by abandoning the traditional policy of abstention from the Dáil. He has always claimed never to have been a member of the IRA, a claim that many have found hard to credit, but there was no doubting his intellect, his skill in debate and his charismatic media presence.

Gerry Adams.

His principal lieutenant was Martin McGuinness from Derry. He had never denied his IRA membership – he had been senior officer in the city in the early days of the Troubles – and was also a competent media performer. He had less electoral success than Adams, failing to dislodge John Hume from his Derry seat. Nonetheless, he established himself on merit as Adams's right-hand man. Charming and polite, he was a formidable politician. Between them, Adams and McGuinness now steered the party slowly towards a political solution.

Loughgall

RUC Crois observation tower.

On 8 May 1987, the IRA suffered its worst military loss of the entire conflict. Eight of its members were shot dead in an attack on the RUC station at Loughgall, County Armagh, the village where the Orange Order had been founded in 1795. A stolen mechanical digger with a large 90-kg/200-lb bomb in its bucket crashed through the station's perimeter defences and destroyed part of the building. But, unknown to the IRA, intelligence reports had betrayed the attack. Forty members of the SAS stationed themselves in the building and adjacent woodland and opened fire, discharging about 1,200 rounds in all.

Eight IRA men died, all members of the very active East Tyrone unit. A passing civilian was caught in the crossfire and also died. The SAS sustained no casualties. After the firefight, they were winched out by helicopter. Triumphant, the RUC put the captured IRA weapons on display the next day.

Ballistic tests demonstrated that these same weapons had been used in 33 previous criminal offences, including murder. Condemnation came from unexpected quarters as well as predicable ones: the Dublin government of Charles Haughey, usually indulgent of republicanism, blamed the IRA for the incident. Moreover, a feud among elements in the Irish National Liberation Army (INLA), an outfit of republican ultras, had left 16 dead. Arms imports for the IRA were intercepted and other caches found. Militant republicanism was low in the water, even in the eyes of its natural supporters. It was about to go lower.

Mural depicting the members of the Provisional IRA killed at Loughgall, Northern Ireland, by the SAS.

Enniskillen

On Sunday 8 November, the annual Remembrance Day ceremony of commemoration for those who had given their lives in two world wars was about to get under way in Enniskillen, County Fermanagh. As the crowd gathered for what was the most solemn day in the calendar of anyone loyal to the British state, a bomb exploded. It had been left in a disused school building adjacent to the cenotaph. The building collapsed on the assembled crowd. Eleven died and 63 were injured. Among the injured was a local headmaster, who was left in a coma.

Devastation after the bomb attack.

The Enniskillen bomb drew international condemnation, from the White House to the Kremlin and the Vatican. Charles Haughey in Dublin uttered his condemnation in words of obvious anger, shame and sincerity. Gordon Wilson, father of one of the victims, spoke to the media with an unaffected eloquence that moved many – including hardbitten journalists – to tears.

Militant republicanism can take a lot of condemnation but what followed Enniskillen was unprecedented. The atrocity had the odd effect of improving community relations within Northern Ireland in the short run, as most unionists registered the sincerity of nationalist disgust. It undoubtedly helped the faltering first steps by Sinn Féin towards a political accommodation that would hopefully end violence. It was horrible – memorable even in the context of a hopeless, futile and stupid conflict – but out of evil came good. The cenotaph bombing in Enniskillen was a turning point.

The Clinton Centre was built in 2002 on the site of the bomb

Gibraltar

On Sunday 6 March 1988, three members of the IRA were shot dead in Gibraltar. Intelligence had suggested that they were in the colony to plant a car bomb that would explode at the scene of a planned British army parade. All three were known IRA activists, two of whom had done time. Still, they were unarmed when shot dead by the SAS. Moreover, it emerged that they had no bomb in Gibraltar, despite early British government claims to the contrary. A second car contained bomb-making equipment and a third, in Marbella, was found to contain plastic explosive. All three cars were linked to the IRA.

Site by Southport Gates in Gibraltar where it was alleged three members of the IRA were planning on detonating a car bomb during a military parade in 1988.

The killings were hugely controversial, for they suggested an overt shoot-to-kill policy, long suspected by republicans and others as part of the British response to IRA provocations. Some British politicians called for an enquiry but Thatcher typically refused. It looked bad, as if the security forces had been dragged down to the IRA's level. The more worldly response was that fire needed to be fought with fire.

The aftermath was awful. The three bodies were brought back to Belfast. A lone loyalist lunatic inveigled his way in to the funeral and threw grenades and fired shots at mourners, killing three. Three days later, at the funeral of one of the three, two British soldiers, who had wandered into the cortège in error – they were lost, being new to Belfast – were pulled out of their car and killed by a mob.

Mural at Tullycarnet on the outskirts of Belfast in support of the East Belfast Brigade, of the UFF/UDA, of which Stone became a member.

Mourners take cover at Milltown cemetery while under attack by loyalist gunman, Michael Stone, Belfast 1988.

Back-Channel Talks

The killings went on, tit for tat. It seemed endless and hopeless. Anglo-Irish relations chilled under the suspicion of a shoot-to-kill policy and London's adamantine refusal to hold an enquiry. The 1985 Anglo-Irish Agreement kept lines of communication open between London, Belfast and Dublin, however fraught. Irish extradition law, long a bone of contention, changed and – very gradually – republicans began being extradited northwards.

Albert Reynolds.

In November, the new secretary of state, Peter Brooke, suggested that the government might consider talking to Sinn Féin if the IRA declared a ceasefire. The reaction, predictably, was outrage. It does seem likely, however, that some contacts were in place as early as late 1990. Prior to that, John Hume and Gerry Adams had been having secret talks since 1988, with Hume trying to convince Adams of the futility of violence, especially since the advent of the Anglo-Irish Agreement.

In the nature of these things, the details are murky. The general view is that the IRA wanted an out, without surrendering honour as they saw it. In 1993, *The Observer* reported that secret talks had indeed been going on for three years. Haughey and Thatcher had been replaced by Albert Reynolds and John Major, who developed a positive mutual chemistry. Sinn Féin was clearly ascendant within republicanism, with ever more stress on politics. The stars seemed to be aligning at long last.

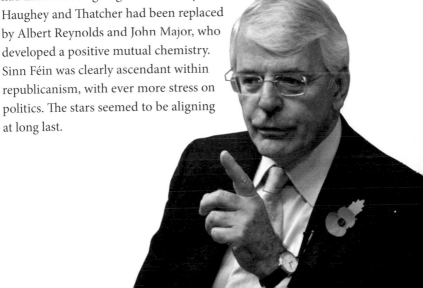

John Major speaking at Chatham House, London.

The Downing Street Declaration

In December 1993, Major and Reynolds issued a joint declaration on Northern Ireland. It was a document of considerable subtlety, as it had to be. It declared that the British government had 'no selfish or strategic interest in Northern Ireland', which sounded like a dilution of the constitutional guarantee but wasn't: it was a statement of the obvious. Constitutionally, it meant nothing in the moment but it left an ambiguous door open for ultimate withdrawal if the circumstances were to warrant it. On the other hand, Dublin accepted that Irish self-determination was a matter for the Irish people and that London acknowledged this, but that any such self-determination could only operate in the context of a majority in Northern Ireland desiring it. That was a retreat from the blunt territorial claim in articles 2 and 3 of the Irish constitution.

Instead of emphasising the territorial integrity of the island – long a republican and nationalist axiom – what mattered now was an 'agreed Ireland', which both governments resolved to facilitate as best they could. All in all, it was an exemplary exercise in constructive ambiguity. Dublin displayed a degree of sensitivity to unionist concerns hitherto absent and promised changes to some of its own more sectarian laws. London kept influential unionists involved in the drafting process, thus avoiding the over-their-heads deal as in 1985.

Accordingly, James Molyneaux, the leader of the Ulster Unionist Party, was able to endorse the declaration, in sharp contrast to his outrage over the Anglo-Irish Agreement eight years earlier. Paisley, naturally, howled betrayal and some republican activists were decidedly sceptical. Yet Adams was now steering the republican ship with some skill and in one direction only.

Prime Minister John Major shakes hands with An Taoiseach Albert Reynolds outside 10 Downing Street in 1993.

The IRA Ceasefire

Despite all this, the violence did not stop in 1994. Adams told a Sinn Féin ard fheis that the Downing Street Declaration was a positive step but one that left many critical issues unaddressed. Then, at the end of August, the long-desired announcement came: 'Recognising the potential of the current situation and in order to enhance the democratic peace process ... the leadership of [the IRA] have decided that as of midnight, Wednesday, 31 August, there will be a complete cessation of military operations.'

IRA ceasefire September 1994 wall mural.

Inevitably, nationalists were jubilant and unionists sceptical. There were things left unsaid in the IRA statement, which was hardly a surprise. Such things remained to be resolved at what were now clearly political negotiations to come.

Gerry Adams in New York.

Two major issues were to dog the talks that did eventuate: the release of 'political' prisoners and the surrender or decommissioning of illegal arms. Adams had admitted the importance of decommissioning in an earlier media interview but he backtracked hastily thereafter.

One controversial move arising from the ceasefire was to prove significant in the years to come. Gerry Adams was granted a visa to enter the United States, contrary to the representations of the British government. Unionist anxiety now focused on the danger of a potent pan-nationalist coalition, comprising the northern minority, the Dublin government and the Irish-American diaspora.

Above all, the ceasefire demonstrated the sheer good sense of the Anglo-Irish Agreement of 1985. Dublin had to be a player in any settlement, holding – as it did – the allegiance of nearly 40 per cent of the population of Northern Ireland.

The Loyalist Ceasefire

The IRA ceasefire was followed in short order by a similar announcement from the loyalists. The Combined Loyalist Military Command (CLMC) was an umbrella group embracing the UVF, the UFF and the Red Hand Commandos. Their announcement read: 'After having received confirmation and guarantees in relation to Northern Ireland's constitutional position within the United Kingdom ... the CLMC will universally cease all operational hostilities from 12 midnight on Thursday 13 October 1994.'

David Ervine was a Northern Irish unionist politician from Belfast and the leader of the Progressive Unionist Party. He was a member of the Ulster Volunteer Force (UVF) during his youth and was imprisoned for possessing bomb-making equipment. Ervine helped to deliver the loyalist ceasefire of 1994.

As with republicanism, loyalism was beginning to generate political animals to substitute for the psychopathic ones that had been their previous trademark. Their ceasefire was unsurprisingly predicated on a continuation of the IRA one but they also offered an apology to the families of their victims over many years. The families might have been forgiven any scepticism, but it was at least a gesture – well regarded at the time.

Just as Adams was moving republicanism to a more nuanced position, loyalist politicians were likewise beginning to move their people towards some sort of accommodation and understanding of the other side. In this regard, the outstanding talent was David Ervine. Back in 1975, he had been sentenced to 11 years in prison for transporting a bomb for the UVF. Now, 20 years later, he began a political career that demonstrated a subtle and patient intelligence in the face of the inevitable provocations and difficulties still ahead. Tragically, he was to die young – genuinely mourned on all sides – but while he lived he played his full part in the denouement to come.

Mural celebrating former Progressive Unionist Party leader David Ervine, Montrose Street South, Albertbridge Road, East Belfast.

Drumcree

In April 1995, the Northern Ireland Office announced that ministers would begin exploratory talks with Sinn Féin. This soon developed into multi-party talks. Then, like a malign ghost, one of the province's least appealing problems re-appeared.

For many years, the Orange Order's annual march in Portadown had been routed along the nationalist Garvaghy Road on their return from a service in nearby Drumcree church. The marchers claimed to be merely asserting their right to walk the queen's highway; the

A mural supporting the Portadown Orangemen, Lower Shankill, Belfast.

nationalists saw it as coat-trailing. In 1995, there was a stand-off and the marchers got through only after an ambiguous compromise between marchers and residents. Some claimed that the Orangemen had promised to take an alternative route in 1996. They did not, and widespread disruption spread throughout the province. Unionist parties withdrew from the Stormont talks. The police originally banned the march from the Garvaghy Road before reversing the decision as the least-worst option. This prompted rioting in Catholic areas. In 1997, police and the army threw a 'ring of steel' around the town and sealed off the Garvaghy Road, along which the Orangemen processed silently. More riots followed. In 1998, under new legislation, the parade was finally rerouted, sparking riots in Protestant areas.

There were deaths, including those of three Catholic children in a sectarian attack in County Antrim, together with further riots, disorders, house-burnings and general mayhem – all stemming from the Drumcree stand-off. But the legislative changes and the establishment of a parades commission to decide parade routes gradually drew the sting of the protest, which petered out from 2001 onwards without ever quite disappearing. The whole situation indicated how intractable the issues were in Northern Ireland and how much difficulty lay in the way of a political resolution.

David Trimble

Lord David Trimble.

David Trimble was a barrister and law lecturer who had been elected to Westminster as MP for the Upper Bann constituency in 1990. Portadown was in the heart of his constituency and when the Drumcree stand-off began, he took the side of the Orangemen along with Ian Paisley. This first brought him to public notice. A month later, when the leadership of the UUP fell open after the resignation of James Molyneaux, Trimble won the nomination. He was now the leader of the largest unionist party, a successor to Craigavon, Brookeborough and Faulkner.

Trimble talked tough, adopting hardline positions. At the same time, he did things not previously associated with unionist leaders. He visited President Clinton in the White House and called on Government Buildings in Dublin, which

was a first. He tried without success to insist on
IRA decommissioning of arms prior to substantive
negotiations. While trying to contain the passions of
his fractious base, he nonetheless steered mainstream
unionism along a less confrontational path.

He was central to the successful outcome of the
Belfast Agreement of 1998 and became first minister
of the devolved administration that followed. He
and John Hume jointly won the Nobel Peace
Prize for their efforts. Eventually, both
winners would be marginalised as events
in the early 21st century conspired
to bring the unionist and nationalist
extremes closer in a most improbable
alliance. But Trimble, a cultured and
cultivated man, showed considerable
courage and no little political skill in
helping to make a decisive
breakthrough in 1998.

John Hume.

Bill Clinton in Northern Ireland

Clinton showed a greater engagement with Northern Ireland than any United States president before him. He called a conference on trade and investment and pledged up to $30m for the International Fund for Ireland. Crucially, as it transpired, he appointed the former United States Senate majority leader George Mitchell to be special economic adviser on Ireland. Mitchell, who would display the patience of Job in chairing the talks that finally delivered the Belfast Agreement of 1998, was quietly inspirational.

Clinton then became the first American President since Eisenhower to visit Northern Ireland. He came for one day in November 1995. He visited both the Falls and Shankill Roads, shook hands with Gerry Adams (thus dismissing another taboo), made speeches, popped over to Derry before returning to Belfast to switch on the Christmas tree lights outside City Hall. Clinton had the charisma of a rock star. In all, he spoke to more than 150,000 people during

Bill Clinton.

U.S. Special Envoy
George Mitchell.

his day in Northern Ireland, spent the night in the Europa Hotel – the most bombed hotel in Europe – and the next day addressed a crowd of 100,000 in Dublin plus the joint houses of the Oireachtas.

To get from there to the Belfast Agreement three years later involved a lot of heavy lifting. There were terrible moments, which might have prompted everyone to walk away from what might justifiably have been regarded as a hopeless enterprise. But the stolid presence of the president of the United States in the background – acting like a political lender of last resort – was a critical element in the outcome.

President Bill Clinton, Prime Minster Tony Blair, David Trimble, Seamus Mallon and Lord Mayor David Alderdice addressing the Assembly of Northern Ireland in the main auditorium at Waterfront Hall in Belfast, Northern Ireland.

The IRA Ceasefire Ends

It was not plain sailing in the latter half of the 1990s. In February 1997, the IRA announced the end of its ceasefire. They claimed that the British government and the unionists had acted in bad faith in failing to advance the peace process to the complete satisfaction of the IRA. In fact, it was a cynical tactic to increase the pressure. A bomb exploded in an underground car park in Canary Wharf in London, killing two men, injuring hundreds and causing over £100m worth of damage.

The British government and the unionists wanted a republican commitment on decommissioning of arms prior to any substantive talks. This was reasonable but unrealistic. George Mitchell, in the first of many key interventions, persuaded London to drop this. Trimble then took the initiative by proposing the election of a special Northern Ireland assembly to enable a negotiated settlement. London endorsed this idea, as some republicans also appeared to do. This was a new departure: a unionist leader showing some initiative rather than just saying 'no' to everything.

The assembly elections produced 30 UUP members, 24 DUP, 21 SDLP, 17 Sinn Féin and various others. Talks were predictably difficult, not least concerning the end of the ceasefire and the continuing stand-off at Drumcree. Tony Blair's landslide win in the 1997 UK general election and the arrival of Mo Mowlam – a straight-talking, no-nonsense woman – as Northern Ireland secretary of state pushed things forward. London no longer insisted on decommissioning. Instead a return to the ceasefire was the only requirement for Sinn Féin to enter talks. It duly came in July 1997.

The Right Honourable Mo Mowlam. She was MP for Redcar from 1987 to 2001 and served in the Cabinet as Secretary of State for Northern Ireland, Minister for the Cabinet Office and Chancellor of the Duchy of Lancaster. The Good Friday Peace Agreement was signed in 1998. She was popular for her personal charisma and plain speaking.

The Belfast Agreement

In September, Sinn Féin signed the Mitchell Principles – which committed all parties to peaceful means, verifiable disarmament and a commitment to abide by any agreement reached – and entered the talks. The UUP, DUP and fringe loyalists walked out. All stayed out except the UUP, who returned after a short interval, their point made.

The talks that eventually led to the Belfast Agreement were protracted, full of suspicion and mistrust on all sides, almost derailed by maddening quibbles – and yet they succeeded. For this, it is hard to know where the primary credit lies. The Americans, especially Mitchell, kept the show on the road. Tony Blair threw his now considerable authority behind a deal. Likewise, An Taoiseach Bertie Ahern, a brilliant negotiator, deserves every credit. Adams and McGuinness demonstrated their worth, and John Hume could feel vindicated by the eventual agreement, of which he might claim to have been intellectual godfather. Trimble was heroic: he held the weakest hand and played it with a cool head.

The bones of the agreement are these: the constitutional position of Northern Ireland was unchanged; Dublin accepted this and resolved to remove the territorial claim from its constitution, which it did; there was to be a power-sharing executive in Belfast and cross-border cooperation on matters of mutual interest; 'political prisoners' were to be released and decommissioning was promised, but fudged.

Seamus Mallon, Hume's number two in the SDLP, famously called it Sunningdale for slow learners. It was a very substantial achievement, despite the fudge, which was almost inevitable in any settlement that required constructive ambiguity.

L-R: Tony Blair, Martin McGuinness, David Trimble, John Hume, Gerry Adams and Bertie Ahern.

The Assembly Elections

The Belfast Agreement found overwhelming favour among nationalists on both sides of the border. As with Sunningdale back in 1974, however, unionists were much more sceptical. Many saw it as a surrender to the IRA, with the key question of decommissioning left hanging on Sinn Féin's promises, which were to prove hard to cash in. In particular, the sight of killers and criminals walking out of jails disgusted many unionists, who wondered if the agreement had been bought at too high a price. Among those released were the Balcombe Street Gang, who were given a rapturous heroes' reception at a Sinn Féin ard fheis. It was a crass and stupid demonstration of where republican hearts truly lay.

The Belfast Agreement was approved by 71.1 per cent of Northern Ireland in a referendum. Assuming near-total approval of nationalists, the margin indicated the divisions and doubts within unionism. The assembly elections produced a solid pro-agreement majority: 80 for and 28 against, so that a power-sharing executive became a practical proposition.

It had taken a mighty effort of persuasion on behalf of the British government and the Americans to persuade enough unionists to support the agreement. The chancellor, Gordon Brown, announced a 'peace through prosperity' economic stimulus to the value of £350m. At the same time, Blair spoke out of both sides of his mouth at once. At a meeting in one (Protestant) secondary school, a clever pupil asked him how his promise to republicans that the agreement represented the start of the road to unification could be reconciled with his assurance to unionists that it protected Northern Ireland's existing constitutional position. Answer came there none from the prime minister.

Gordon Brown.

Tony Blair.

Omagh

For all the doubts about the new arrangements on the unionist sides, it was a republican atrocity of exceptional horror that reminded people of how fragile the new dispensation was. On 15 August 1998, just months after the agreement was signed, a 125-kg/300-lb bomb was detonated in the centre of the market town of Omagh, County Tyrone, in the middle of a busy afternoon. The town was full of shoppers. There was also a local summer festival in progress, ensuring the presence of many children.

RUC police officers and firefighters inspect the damage caused by a bomb in Market Street, Omagh, County Tyrone, 15 August 1998.

Twenty-nine people died and 360 were injured, many horribly mutilated. It was probably the most shocking atrocity since Enniskillen. It was claimed by a dissident republican outfit styling themselves as the Real IRA. They were unrepentant, saying that they had given a warning to the RUC. They had, but it had been ambiguous, and the result was that the police mistakenly directed people towards the bomb rather than away from it. The Real IRA continued: ' … it was not our intention at any time to kill civilians. It was a commercial target, part of an ongoing war against the Brits. We offer apologies to the civilians.'

As usual with militant republicans, it was never their fault. Amazingly, this ghastly atrocity did not derail the peace process. Instead, the INLA – another gang of republican firebrands – announced a ceasefire. Martin McGuinness was appointed to liaise with the decommissioning commission. Trimble and Adams met face to face at Stormont. It was hardly business as usual, but everyone was trying to go the extra mile.

This chilling photograph taken in the minutes before the explosion was found by investigators in a camera buried in the rubble.

The Northern Ireland Executive

The violence did not stop but it abated. Fifty-five people died in incidents relating to the Troubles in 1998 – including the 29 at Omagh – compared to 84 five years earlier and 94 in 1988. On 1 July, the new assembly met for the first time and an executive was formed. David Trimble (UUP) became first minister and Seamus Mallon (SDLP) his deputy.

David Trimble.

The whole vexed question of decommissioning dragged on, with ever-increasing unionist suspicion of Sinn Féin's good faith. For the moment, they were excluded from executive office on that account. North-south implementation bodies and a cross-border ministerial council were established, albeit later than decreed in the agreement. The DUP remained hostile to the entire new dispensation.

In December, the UUP and the SDLP reached agreement on the structure of the new executive. There were to be ten departments, covering agriculture, the environment, health, education, finance, trade and so on. The big questions, to do with dealings with the Treasury in London and the EU Commission in Brussels were located in the offices of the first minister and his deputy.

The north-south implementation bodies were to deal with inland waterways, food safety, business development, cooperation on EU matters, marine matters and – this would later become a bogey – the Irish and Ulster Scots languages. The headline areas identified for cross-border cooperation included transport and tourism, with provision also made for a north-south ministerial council, a British-Irish council and a civic forum, which would have a consultative role on social, cultural and economic matters.

Seamus Mallon (SDLP) speaking at the John Hewitt International Summer School in 2017.

The Assembly Elections, 2003

One of the key provisions of the Belfast Agreement was police reform, and in due course the RUC mutated into the Police Service of Northern Ireland (PSNI). The reforms were more than cosmetic: the new service aimed at a 50:50 recruitment policy across the sectarian divide; there was a new policing board of 19, of whom ten were assembly members; and there was an ombudsman to deal with complaints.

Sinn Féin's Gerry Adams.

SDLP leader Mark Durkan.

Many unionists saw these reforms as an insult to the RUC, which they had regarded as their shield. Combined with continued foot-dragging on decommissioning, unionist support for the Belfast Agreement weakened. Some progress was made on decommissioning but not enough. An important prompt came from the United States, no longer indulgent of faraway terrorism in the wake of 9/11.

The assembly was briefly prorogued in 2000 because of the

decommissioning stand-off, and Trimble resigned as first minister on the same issue in 2001. The DUP now entered the process by taking up ministerial positions and sitting on committees but declined to sit on the executive itself.

These shifts and eddies were made clear in the results of the assembly election for 2003. For the first time, the DUP passed out the UUP to become the largest unionist party: 25.6 per cent to 22.7 per cent. Even more dramatic was the eclipse of the SDLP by Sinn Féin. They had been coming in with the tide for some time. Now they pulled clear, winning 23.5 per cent of the vote to the SDLP's 17 per cent. Each tribe was retreating towards its bunker.

Alliance leader David Ford and colleagues at the launch of his party's election manifesto in East Belfast.

The UK General Election, 2005

The decommissioning saga dragged on, as reluctant progress was made. Independent observers verified that three arms caches had been 'put beyond use', and in January 2004 an independent monitoring commission was established. Then two things happened in quick succession. In December 2004, a huge robbery at the Northern Bank in central Belfast netted £26.5m for the thieves, almost certainly republicans. It was the biggest bank robbery in UK history. Then, the following month, Robert McCartney, a Catholic, was murdered in broad daylight in a Belfast pub. It was a conventional pub row but there were republican figures involved. The pub was forensically 'cleaned' to destroy evidence while rioters kept the PSNI at bay. It was clear that militant republicanism and its supporters were still alive and well.

All this further eroded unionist confidence in the post-agreement arrangements. Still, the results of the UK general election of 2005 were startling. The DUP were not now just ahead of the UUP: they were out of sight. They received 33.7 per cent of votes cast to the UUP's 17.7 per cent, a low from which the UUP have never recovered. Indeed, they went on to lose a further share in the following years, yielding the unionist ground decisively to Paisley's party.

On the nationalist side, Sinn Féin slightly increased its lead over the SDLP, but for the latter the same fate awaited as that of the UUP. The next ten years brought steady decline, as Sinn Féin became the leading voice on its side of the divide.

Arlene Foster is leader of the Democratic Unionist Party (DUP) and member of the Northern Ireland Assembly since 2003. In 2016, Foster became First Minister of Northern Ireland and shared power with Martin McGuinness.

Nigel Dodds is a Northern Irish barrister and unionist politician. He is MP for Belfast North, and deputy leader of the DUP since June 2008.

The St Andrew's Agreement

Out of this calculus, there emerged the most improbable concurrence in the entire story. Both the London and Dublin governments recognised the new electoral reality in Northern Ireland and effectively began to abandon the UUP and the SDLP as no longer up to the job. They produced a set of joint proposals to see if the DUP and Sinn Féin could cooperate in a revised set of devolved structures. The DUP would have to agree to share power with Sinn Féin and they, in turn, would have to recognise the legitimacy of the PSNI. Astonishingly, these things happened. The DUP pretended that St Andrew's was a whole new deal – this was to gull their supporters. In fact, it was simply a re-tread.

It worked. The IRA put out a statement to say that its campaign was finally over for good, although dissidents remained on the margin. A new executive was formed in 2007 with Ian Paisley as first minister and Martin McGuinness as his deputy. After a year in the sunshine at last, the ageing Paisley handed over to his party deputy, Peter Robinson. In a move of the greatest possible significance, army support for the police was withdrawn as being no longer necessary, and by April 2010 security powers were fully devolved.

It was as if normal was the new normal. Belfast city centre began a wonderful transformation from a bashed-about wreck of a place to a confident, prosperous provincial city. It was symbolised by the opening of the Titanic Centre in 2012 on the centenary of the sinking of that famous ship built by Harland & Wolff in its glory days. It has been a stunning success.

The Titanic Centre, Belfast.

The Chuckle Brothers

Back in the early 1990s, the mutual regard that John Major and Albert Reynolds had for each other helped pave the way for the Downing Street Declaration. This kind of positive inter-personal chemistry is often overlooked in political analysis: it matters more than many think. However, has there ever been a more improbable double act than Ian Paisley and Martin McGuinness? Each had no shortage of charm, but it was generally reserved for persons of their own persuasion. Each had been at the far margin of his political community. Now they were in government together.

It was clear that on a personal level they discovered that they liked each other. There is a famous photograph of the pair of them laughing their heads off, obviously enjoying each other's company. It won them the sobriquet of 'the Chuckle Brothers', after an English children's comedy act of the same name.

It is not as if all problems had been solved. Tensions and differences still persisted, in areas such as schooling, health and the economic response to the financial crash of 2008. An agreed community relations policy remained as elusive as ever. Moreover, Northern Ireland was ludicrously over-represented with politicians: a population of 1.8m people had an assembly of 108 members, roughly double the representation of Scotland or the Republic of Ireland by population. Still, perhaps better to have too much politics than too little. Northern Ireland had learned that the hard way.

Ian Paisley and Martin McGuinness.

Stand-Off

The years after the 2008 financial crisis were as tough on Northern Ireland as everywhere else. London, which completely controlled the province's purse strings, introduced a series of austerity measures that Sinn Féin, in particular, had difficulty selling to its members. However, the system carried on, punctuated by things like the Stormont House Agreement of 2014, which ticked off a lot of relatively uncontentious issues while leaving the more incendiary ones, such as the Irish language question, undisturbed.

Opinion polls showed diminishing public confidence in the assembly. This was reflected in declining turnouts in elections, although that may be accounted for in part by Northern Ireland seeming to have an interminable series of these, at national, provincial and local levels. An assembly election in 2016 maintained the new party proportions. Arlene Foster replaced Robinson as first minister but was soon caught up in a scandal over a Renewable Heat Incentive scheme, known colloquially as Cash for Ash, which failed at a likely cost to the public purse of somewhere between £400m and £500m.

Foster had been the line minister responsible for this debacle. Her deputy, Martin McGuinness, resigned, thus collapsing the executive.

(It was a requirement that it must contain both a first minister and a deputy.) Moreover, McGuinness was in declining health and died in 2017. Sinn Féin refused to replace him. Thus ended devolution for the moment. At the time of writing, the institutions are still in abeyance.

Michelle O'Neill replaced McGuinness as Sinn Féin's leader in the Northern Ireland Assembly in January 2017.

Stasis

The assembly election of 2017 showed the DUP barely ahead of Sinn Féin, with no overall unionist majority. The demographic time bomb – unionism's worst nightmare – was ticking. The 2011 census had shown that Catholics, with their higher birth rate, were now 45 per cent of Northern Ireland's population, as against 48 per cent of Protestants. A small but growing immigrant community further confused these figures: the census showed their numbers at 81,000, three times the figure for 2001.

However, headlines about growing Catholic numbers can be misleading. A BBC opinion survey in 2013 showed a small but telling majority of Catholics wishing to stay in the UK. The nationalist demographic dream, of Northern Ireland suddenly having a Catholic majority, might happen, but it is far from clear if that would mean the end of partition.

Aerial view of Lough Melvin, overlooking Leitrim, Donegal and Fermanagh, the border between Northern Ireland and Ireland.

A poll conducted by the *Irish Times* in early 2019 similarly showed a majority still in favour of retaining the constitutional attachment to the United Kingdom. The margin was 45 per cent to 32 per cent, with each choice heavily weighted, as one might expect, towards one community or the other. Interestingly, the don't knows in that survey amounted to 23 per cent, with Protestants and Catholics much closer together on this metric than on a definite choice one way or the other.

This uncertainty and confusion was caused by a number of factors, not least demography. But most of all, the great destabiliser was the political bomb that exploded in June 2016, when the UK voted by plebiscite to leave the EU.

Bullet-riddled sign on the border between Northern Ireland and the Republic of Ireland.

Anti-Brexit poster

Border poll sign.

Brexit

England and Wales voted to leave the EU. Scotland was firmly against the proposal, as was Northern Ireland. There, the vote to remain was 56 per cent. The remain vote was substantially nationalist, although some unionist commercial and agricultural interests appear to have chosen remain out of concern for the economic upheaval that Brexit might entail.

Brexit cannot be wholly disentangled from the Scottish demand for independence. A referendum on that question was defeated by 55 to 45 per cent in 2015, but the Scottish Brexit vote has inevitably reopened the matter. Were Scotland to vote again on the issue, as seems quite possible, and this time choose independence within the EU, it would mean the end of the United Kingdom. The implications for Northern Ireland are obvious – and at the same time hard to calculate.

The Brexit negotiations have been handled with the greatest incompetence by the Conservative government of Theresa May. In all this, Northern Ireland is a passive agent. Its future is not in its own hands; the only certainty is uncertainty. A secretary of state, Karen Bradley, was despatched to Belfast where she demonstrated an astonishing degree of ignorance about the sectarian and political realities of the province. Relations with Dublin have chilled because the Republic wants guarantees that, in the event of Britain leaving the EU, there will be no 'hard border' in Ireland. That will be difficult to avoid if the UK exits the EU customs union. But a hard border is an invitation to trouble – or should that be Troubles?

Mural on houses in Derry.

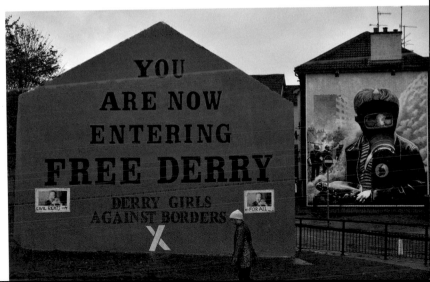

Milkman & Derry Girls

So much of the story of Northern Ireland has been one of hopelessly divided loyalties; a polity that cannot function for want of a governing consensus; a divided population that, now as much as ever, is a kind of informal apartheid society: different schools, different sports, different housing districts. The dismal pattern of civic disorder, mayhem and murder – driven by ethno-religious hatreds – has abated without dying out. Who would bet against a revival of the old ways? There are dissident militants on both sides of the divide who would be glad of an excuse to make trouble. Brexit offers dissident republicans – those utterly irreconcilable fanatics who murdered a young journalist in Derry in April 2019 – a free lunch.

Lyra McKee was a prominent Northern Irish journalist who wrote for several publications about the Troubles. On 18 April 2019, McKee was fatally shot during rioting in the Creggan area of Derry. Police blamed dissident republicans for her death.

But there is another side to the story. In the years of the Troubles, this little spot of earth has produced Seamus Heaney, Derek Mahon, Michael Longley and a host of other poets of quality. It has produced novelists of distinction, as well as some of the finest journalism to come from anywhere in that time. In 2018, Anna Burns, originally from Belfast, won the Man Booker Prize, the UK's leading award for literary fiction, for her novel *Milkman*.

And then there is the phenomenon known as *Derry Girls*. A television comedy written by Lisa McGee and set in Northern Ireland in the 1990s, it has been a runaway success both with the public and the critics. The show won the IFTA Gala TV Award for best comedy in 2018; McGee won the best screenwriter award. Let's end there, in the hope that that is the future and that the past can be buried.

Stars of the Channel 4 comedy series *Derry Girls* depicted in a mural. The painting was created by UV Arts C.I.C. It stretches almost ten metres high across the side of Badger's Pub, Derry.

Select bibliography

Bardon, Jonathan, *A History of Ulster*, Belfast 1992

Bew, Paul & Gillespie, Gordon, *Northern Ireland: a chronology of the Troubles 1968–99*, Dublin 1999

Connolly, Seán, ed., *The Oxford Companion to Irish History*, Oxford 1998

Elliott, Marianne, *The Catholics of Ulster: a history*, London 2000

Flackes, W.D. & Elliott, Sydney, *Northern Ireland: a political directory 1968–99*, Belfast 1999

Hennessey, Thomas, *A History of Northern Ireland 1920-96*, Dublin 1997

McKay, Susan, *Northern Protestants: an unsettled people*, Belfast 2000

Toolis, Kevin, *Rebel Hearts: journeys within the IRA's soul*, London 1995

Picture credits

The publisher gratefully acknowledges the following image copyright holders. All images are copyright © individual rights holders unless stated otherwise. Every effort has been made to trace copyright holders, or copyright holders not mentioned here. If there have been any errors or omissions, the publisher would be happy to rectify this in any reprint.

p3 Rijksmuseum/Wiki/CC
p7 Teapot Press
p8 Rijksmuseum/Wiki/CC
p9 Teapot Press
p11 Teapot Press
p12 Teapot Press
p13 Teapot Press
p14 NPG London
p15 LoC
p16 Teapot Press
p17 Wikipedia/CC
p18 Wikipedia/CC
p19 Wikipedia/CC
p20 Teapot Press
p21 Wikipedia/CC
p22 Unknown
p23 W.D. Hogan/NLI/CC
p25 Teapot Press
p26 Wiki/CC
p27 Wiki/CC
p27 Teapot Press
p28 Wiki/CC
p29 Unknown
p30 LoC
p31 Flickr
p32 Teapot Press
p33 De Luan/Alamy
p34 Unknown
p36 Unknown
p37 NPG London
p38 NLI @ Flickr /CC
p41 NLI @ Flickr /CC
p43 Mick Harper/Shutterstock
p44 NPG London
p46 Unknown
p47 Unknown
p49 Teapot Press
p50 Wikipedia
p51 NPG London
p52 Science History Images/Alamy
p55 Flickr/Billy Black/CC

p57 LoC
p58 Wiki/CC
p59 NPG London
p60 Wiki/CC
p60 NPG London
p61 HMSO/Wiki
p63 Teapot Press
p64 NI Public Records/Flickr
p66 German Federal Archive/Wiki/CC
p67 Unknown
p67 Seán McLaughlin/Derry Journal
p68 NPG London
p69 Wiki/CC/Yousuf Karsh
p70 Chronicle/Alamy
p71 Agence Rol
p73 Wiki/CC
p74 Unknown
p75 PRONI/Flickr/CC
p77 The Picture Art Collection/Alamy
p79 Unknown
p80 Wiki/CC
p81 Wiki/CC
p82 UN Photo/Teddy Chen
p83 Wiki
p84 Isaac Newton/CC
p85 Unknown
p86 Ardfern/Wiki/CC
p87 Teapot Press
p87 Teapot Press
p88 Wiki/CC
p89 Ross/CC
p90 Wiki
p91 Wiki/Vintagekits/
p91 Miss Fitz/Wiki
p91 Wiki/CC
p94 Nationaal Archief/Spaarnestad Photo

p95 Unkown
p96 UUC Yearbook
p96 Patriarchate of Venezia
p97 Keystone Press/Alamy
p98 BHPA, Boston
p99 Alan Mc
p99 Dan Merino/Flickr/CC
p100 Unknown
p101 Brian O'Neill/Wiki/CC
p102 US National Archives
p103 Keystone Press/Alamy
p104 BHPA, Boston
p105 Derry Sinn Féin/Flickr/CC
p106 Teapot Press
p107 Unknown
p109 Image courtesy RTÉ Archives
p110 Unknown
p112 UUC Yearbook
p113 Trinity Mirror/Mirrorpix/Alamy
p115 Image courtesy RTÉ Archives
p117 Poster Workshop
p118 Keystone Press/Alamy
p121 David Vine
p122 Nationaal Archief/Spaarnestad Photo
p123 Poster Workshop
p124 Unknown
p125 Poster Workshop
p126 Keystone Press/Alamy
p127 Wiki/CC

p128 UN Photo/Teddy Chen
p129 Image courtesy RTÉ Archives
p131 Trinity Mirror/Mirrorpix/Alamy
p132 An Phoblacht
p133 CAIN
p133 Gerry Collins/Belfast Archive Project
p134 Wiki/CC
p135 Trinity Mirror/Mirrorpix/Alamy
p137 John White/Belfast Archive Project
p138 Unknown
p139 Frankie Quinn/Belfast Archive Project
p141 Irish Eye/Alamy
p145 Victor Patterson
p147 Wiki/CC
p148 Wiki/CC/R.Ó Murchú
p150 Unknown
p151 Wiki/CC/Barryob
p152 BHPA, Boston
p153 Ardfern, Creative Commons
p154 Joost Vers/Anefo/Nationaal Archief
p155 Nationaal Archief, Spaarnestad Photo
p156 Wiki
p157 BHPA, Boston
p158 Trinity Mirror/Mirrorpix/Alamy
p159 Keystone Press/Alamy
p161 Trinity Mirror/Mirrorpix/Alamy

p163 Keystone Press/Alamy
p164 Ardfern/CC
p167 Trinity Mirror/Mirrorpix/Alamy
p168 Wiki/CC/Andy Dingley
p169 Alain Le Garsmeur "The Troubles" Archive/Alamy
p170 Keystone Press/Alamy
p172 Teapot Press
p173 Wiki/CC
p174 Teapot Press
p177 Keystone Press/Alamy
p178 Trinity Mirror/Mirrorpix/Alamy
p181 Shutterstock/Nigel Stripe
p183 Shutterstock/Attila Jandi
p185 Keystone Press/Alamy
p186 Trinity Mirror/Mirrorpix/Alamy
p187 Wiki/CC/Brian O'Neill
p188 Peter Denton/Flickr/CC
p189 Open Media Ltd/CC
p191 Keystone Press/Alamy
p192 Unknown
p193 Wiki/Rijksmuseum Amsterdam
p194 Unknown
p195 Image courtesy RTÉ Archives
p197 Wikimedia/CC
p198 Irish Fireside/Flickr/CC
p199 Unknown

p199 Wiki/Allan Warren/CC
p200 Wiki/CC
p210 CAIN
p202 John Farrier/Picturing Icons
p204 Chris Collins/Margaret Thatcher Foundation
p204 Open Media Ltd/CC
p205 Chris McAndrew/CC
p205 Wiki/Mr Penguin
p207 Image courtesy RTÉ Archive
p208 Irish Times
p209 Sinn Féin/Flickr/CC
p210 Wiki/CC
p211 Wiki/CC
p212 Wiki/unknown
p212 Dean Molyneaux/CC
p214 Wiki/CC/Gibmetal77
p215 Mike Abrahams/Alamy
p215 Wiki/CC/Kerespasa
p216 Wiki/CC/Donal/Kinsella
p217 John/Major/Chatham House/CC
p219 Trinity Mirror/Mirrorpix/Alamy
p220 Trinity Mirror/Mirrorpix/Alamy
p221 Gerry Adams/Irish News Archive
p222 BHPA, Boston
p223 Wiki/CC/Kerespasa
p224 Wiki/CC

p226 Chris McAndrew/CC
p227 Wiki/CC
p228 LoC
p228 Wiki/CC
p229 Imago Europe Collection/Alamy
p231 NPG London
p235 IMF/CC
p235 Wiki/CC
p236 Paul McErlane/Alamy
p237 Unknown
p238 Flickr/CC
p239 Alan/Mebham/CC
p240 Sinn Féin/Flickr/CC
p240 Flickr/CC
p241 Flickr/CC
p243 Chris McAndrew/UK Parliament/CC
p243 Frank-Jurgen Richter/Flickr/CC
p245 Wiki/CC/HDR
p247 Stephen Barnes/Politics/Alamy
p249 Sinn Féin/CC
p250 Shutterstock/Ian Mitchinson
p251 Shutterstock/John & Penny
p252 Flickr/CC/Tiocfaidh ar la 1916
p252 Flickr/CC/Tiocfaidh ar la 1916
p253 Flickr/CC/Tiocfaidh ar la 1916
p254 Wiki/CC/International Journalism Festival, Perugia, Italia
p255 Allan Leonard@MrUlster

Abbreviations – BHPA Boston: Bobbie Hanvey Photographic Archives, Boston College. John J. Burns Library / CC: Creative Commons / NPG: National Portrait Gallery LoC: Library of Congress. **Cover images:** Nationaal Archief/Allan Leonard/BHPA/David Vine/Flickr CC Tiocfaidh ar la 1916/Dutch Archive/Derry Sinn Féin CC/NPG Wiki CC/Alamy/Int. Journalism Festival CC/Shutterstock/Unknown/Alamy/Wiki CC/Sinn Féin CC/Teapot Press/Frank-Jurgen Flickr CC/Wiki/Teapot Press/Alamy/Alamy